Roll of Thunder, Hear My Cry

Mildred D. Taylor

D0233745

Guide written by
Stewart Martin

A *Letts* Literature Guide

Extracts from *Roll of Thunder, Hear My Cry* by Mildred D. Taylor are reprinted by kind permission of Victor Gollancz Limited.

First published 1994
Reprinted 1995

Letts Educational
Aldine House, Aldine Place
London W12 8AW

Text © Stewart Martin 1994

Typeset by Jordan Publishing Design

Text Design Jonathan Barnard

Cover and text illustrations Hugh Marshall

Graphic illustration Ian Foulis and Associates

Design © BPP (Letts Educational) Ltd

British Library Cataloguing in Publication Data
A CIP record for this book is available from the British Library

ISBN 1 85758 259 4

Printed and bound in Great Britain by
Ashford Colour Press Ltd, Gosport, Hampshire

Letts Educational is the trading name of BPP (Letts Educational) Ltd

Contents

Plot Synopsis

The story is set in Mississippi, in the Deep South of America, in the 1930s and covers about a year in the life of the Logan family. The Logans are a respectable black family who are much resented, especially by local white landowners, because they own two hundred acres of their own land and are in the process of buying another two hundred. Racial tension runs high in the locality, fuelled mostly by the prejudice of a few white families who see any attempt by the local black farming families to make their way in life as threatening. These local whites still think that it is a white man's world in which 'niggers' should know their place as inferiors. Any suggestion that blacks should be treated in the same way as whites is met with anger or a visit from the feared 'night men' who destroy the property of blacks, or maim and murder them, without being punished. This state of affairs exists even though it is well known which whites are to blame.

The story is told through the eyes of the young Cassie Logan, whose mother teaches at the local all-black school and whose father works away on the railroad for much of each year to raise the money to pay taxes and the mortgage on their land. Cassie and her three brothers help their grandmother, Big Ma, and their mother to farm cotton on their land, from which they make enough money for the family to live on. Cassie's experiences tell us a great deal about what it was like to live as a black family at that time, and we see her mature rapidly as she learns about the cruel ways of the world around her.

The state will not allow blacks to attend the well equipped all-white school and the Logan children are humiliated daily by its bus which threatens their lives and covers them with dust and mud. Eventually the children manage to disable the bus, so that the white children also have to walk to school through the pouring rain and mud. Trouble develops at school when Cassie and her brother protest at being given books which have labels inside showing that the books have been discarded by white students. Their mother, who is regarded as something of a maverick by the other black teachers because of her liberal views, attempts to remedy the situation by pasting paper over the offending pages, but this causes her to be sacked when a black student called T.J., whom she catches cheating in a test, reports her actions to the school board.

The children's father, Papa, returns home and brings his friend, the powerfully built Mr Morrison, to stay with the family and protect them whilst he is away. The night men terrorise a local family, burning one of the men to death and badly scarring two others. Following this the Logan family keep guard during the dark, but the night men frighten the children when they visit the house late one night, even though they go away without taking any action.

Cassie suffers humiliation when she is made to apologise for accidentally bumping into Lillian Jean Simms on the street, but gains her revenge by deliberately becoming the girl's friend and winning her confidence, and then giving her a beating in the forest, after which Cassie threatens to reveal all Lillian Jean's secrets to the other children if she is nasty again. Stacey learns the hard way that gifts should be treasured, when he is persuaded by T.J. to give him the coat which he has been given by his father's brother, Uncle Hammer. Later, T.J. finds himself ignored by the other students because of his unpleasant ways, and he takes to associating with white boys, thinking they are his friends.

The Logans refuse to shop at the local store, knowing that it is run by whites who are members of the night men. When they successfully encourage some other families to join them, Papa and Mr Morrison are ambushed one night and Papa is injured and cannot return to work on the railroad. This means they have less money and the local landowner is suspected of foul play when the bank suddenly call in the Logans' loan on the land. The family are rescued by Uncle Hammer, who sells his car and other possessions to raise the money.

Disaster strikes T.J. as his white 'friends' involve him in the robbery of a store, during which a white man is killed and his wife beaten. The night men track T.J. down after his 'friends' evade punishment by saying that he was involved in the robbery with two other blacks. The night men threaten to hang T.J., as well as Papa and Mr Morrison, but just as it looks as though things will get completely out of hand a fire starts in the cotton fields and everyone rushes to put it out. Later Cassie learns the secret that Papa started the fire and sacrificed some of his own cotton crop in order to stop the mob. Even so, it seems certain to Cassie – who has matured considerably by now – that T.J. will hang for a crime he did not commit.

Chapter 1

Early October 1933
Cassie shows family loyalty and an awareness of injustice when she supports Little Man's rebellion in school.

Chapter 3

Late October
Stacey's wrecking of the school bus shows forethought, courage and determination.

Chapter 5
Cassie learns a lesson about racial inequality. But like Stacey, she will gain her revenge.

Chapter 6
Stacey foolishly gives his overcoat to T.J., but keeps the whistle given him by Jeremy. However, he rejects Jeremy's friendship.

Chapter 8
Harlan Granger gains a partial revenge when Mrs Logan is dismissed from her teaching job – T.J.'s part has not gone unnoticed.

Chapter 9

Spring
T.J., rejected by his friends, seeks the company of R.W. and Melvin.

Chapter 11
R.W. and Melvin set upon T.J. when he falls out with his fellow robbers.

Chapter 11
The lynch mob come for T.J., intending to visit the Logans next.

Chapter 4

Early November

T.J.'s cheating will cause Stacey to suffer – not the last of T.J.'s selfish acts.

Chapter 5

Early November

T.J. wants a gun 'for protection'. Cassie thinks he is foolish. Eventually T.J.'s desires will lead to trouble for them all.

Chapter 7

December

Cassie gains her revenge. She shows care in planning and execution, ensuring that there will be no bad consequences for herself or her family.

Chapter 8

January/February 1934

T.J., angered at his exam failure, criticises Mrs Logan, accusing her of unfairness and of destroying school property.

Chapter 10

Summer

The attack on Mr Logan, Mr Morrison and Stacey leaves Stacey blaming himself and heightens the story's tension.

Chapter 11

One night...Sunday

T.J. gets his gun, but the robbery goes violently wrong with the owners being beaten up.

Chapter 12

Early Monday morning

Mr Logan sets the fields on fire, threatening the crops of white and black alike – T.J.'s fate is postponed.

Chapter 12

Cassie cries for T.J. and the land.

Big Ma and Mrs Logan

These two ladies represent the changing face of the black world through the recent decades.

Big Ma

Big Ma is a strong woman in her sixties and is grandmother to Cassie Logan. She is taller than her daughter-in-law, Mary Logan, and bigger. Her full name is Caroline Logan, but she is usually referred to as Big Ma. In Big Ma's early life it is doubtful that there would have been any opportunity to become a teacher, as her daughter-in-law has done. Her life has been one of hard physical labour, working in the fields with the men. With her husband, she strove hard to keep the land which they had purchased, at the same time as bringing up her children.

As the owner of the Logan land, Big Ma recognises that if she dies Harlan Granger might well attempt to challenge the right of her sons to inherit. Big Ma loves the land probably more than anyone else and she therefore shows a great deal of sense and foresight by arranging to sign papers which give the legal right to the land to her two remaining sons. She has been bothered for years by Harlan Granger, who wants to buy the land back, but the memories which it brings back and the hard work which she has put into it mean far too much to her for that ever to be possible.

Big Ma has a close relationship with her daughter-in-law and grandchildren. Cassie, in particular, relates well to her, though the incident at Strawberry (where Big Ma seems to desert her) causes some resentment for a while. But Big Ma cannot support Cassie against Mr Simms in public without risking violence, any more than she could prevent Mr Andersen from cutting down her trees in the past. Although she is able to use a gun and is prepared to do so to defend her home and family, Big Ma knows the dangers of behaviour that whites will see as provocative, which is why she is so concerned that Hammer might speak out or take action against Mr Simms or the Wallaces.

Mary Logan

Mary Logan is mother to Cassie, Christopher-John, Little Man and Stacey. She is tawny coloured, thin and sinewy with delicate features in a strong-jawed face and is described as being very pretty. She is a good teacher and mother and represents a newly emerging, independent-minded class of blacks. The stand she takes over the matter of the 'new' books demonstrates her attitude to racial equality and her personal integrity. This is also visible when she refuses to alter what she was going to teach when the school board arrive to inspect her, and she has no hesitation in telling Harlan Granger that she will not teach what is in the books about slavery because it is not true. Her action in pasting over the offensive list of names shocks the other teachers. She does not accept that she has a designated 'place' in the world which she must meekly accept and she is a driving force behind the boycott of the Wallace store. She knows that her behaviour threatens her teaching job and that this is important for paying the family's bills, but does not allow this to sway her.

Mary is an understanding and loving mother, but she is also very fair. She almost certainly understands Stacey's innocence over the matter of cheating, but because he would not accuse T.J. she was driven to punish him. In the same way she agrees that Miss Crocker had no alternative but to whip Cassie and Little Man. She explains to Cassie why Big Ma had no choice but to make her apologise to Lillian Jean in Strawberry. Mary also knows that the visit to the badly burnt Mr Berry will do more to convince the children not to visit the Wallace store than any physical punishment.

Mary's relationship with David, her husband, is one of love, mutual trust and support; they are equal partners in bringing up their family and striving to retain their land. She is grateful for Mr Morrison's presence but is anxious that he, like Uncle Hammer, should do nothing to put themselves at risk. She is more conscious of, and more easily frightened by, threats than her husband. It is Mary's desperate pleading to David to find a way to help T.J. without drawing violence down upon themselves, that makes him think twice about what he should do.

David Logan and Uncle Hammer

The adult Logan family: Big Ma, Mary Logan, David and Hammer, are a close-knit group. They are determined to hold on to their hard-won land. Hammer is a resident of the big towns and cities, but he sacrifices all of his possessions to help the family keep the land. David works unceasingly to give the family financial security. Like his wife, Mary, and his mother, Big Ma, he is sensitive to their needs and is caring and totally honest.

David Logan

David Logan is the children's father. Usually they refer to him as Papa. He is 6' 2" tall and the youngest of a family of brothers, two of whom are now dead. There is a striking contrast in character between David and his remaining brother, Hammer. David is tied to the land. His whole life is devoted to ensuring that the family retains the heritage that has been so hard won. He wants his children to inherit what he and his forebears have worked so hard to gain. He is a loving and caring father who is also very strict, as we witness when he punishes the children for their visit to the Wallaces' store. The children always know where they stand with their father and always know that he will treat their concerns seriously. He gives his children advice and helps them to see the importance of making their own decisions and taking the consequences for them, as when he advises Cassie to carefully consider whether seeking revenge on 'Miz' Lillian Jean is worth the risks involved in standing up for a principle. If Papa ever does make it clear that he expects to be obeyed on an issue, the children know better than to argue with him if his mind is made up: 'Papa always meant what he said – and he swung a mean switch'.

David's attitude towards white people is obviously influenced by his own experiences. When Jeremy comes to give Stacey a present, he indicates that Stacey should accept it – he is sensitive to his young visitor's feelings and does not to want to embarrass him. But he also indicates to Stacey that the relationship should not go any further. His suggestion to Stacey that Jeremy might change, and that there is no long-term point in being friends, is a very negative view, but an understandable one. Ironically, the visit from Mr Jamison and his offer to act as guarantor for credit takes both David and his brother by surprise and poses an interesting contrast to David's advice to his son about not trusting white friends.

David Logan shows himself to be a very determined and single-minded man when it comes to keeping hold of the land. Only when his family are at risk does this take second place. In setting fire to the fence he sacrifices a quarter of his cotton crop, but at the same time manages to stop the lynching of T.J. and the imminent attack on his own family.

Uncle Hammer

Uncle Hammer lives in the North where, in theory, blacks are equal to whites and have the same rights. Understandably, therefore, Hammer finds the situation in the South very frustrating and his well-known fiery temper leads the rest of the family to worry about how he will react to events on a number of occasions. Hammer is generous towards the children, but has no sympathy when Stacey allows himself to be swindled out of the new coat which Hammer gives him. Believing that people should accept the responsibility for their own stupidity, Hammer lets T.J. keep the coat as a permanent and painful reminder to Stacey of his own foolishness.

Hammer takes pleasure in reminding the local whites that he considers himself their equal, both by the way he speaks to them and by the way he dresses and behaves. His purchase of a Packard car – identical to (but newer than) Harlan Granger's – is a deliberate act of defiance. His defiance also shows in his desire to seek immediate and violent revenge on local white racists who are known to have killed, hurt or victimised blacks, but each time he is persuaded that this would be dangerous, or he restrains himself from doing anything which might endanger those he cares for. Hammer's love for his family – and his own recognition of the importance of the family's ownership of land – results in him selling his car and his possessions when they most need money.

Cassie

Cassie

The story is told to us by Cassie Logan, who is nine years old when it begins. Because she is the narrator (story-teller) we do not get an outside view of her character and we therefore have to find out most of what we learn about her as a person for ourselves. But Cassie also has a typical nine-year-old's honesty and her straightforward comments about other characters are often very revealing. Her direct and simple questions about things and her resentment at the racial intolerance she sees around her are made sharper for us because they come from a child.

There are occasions when both we and Cassie learn things which we otherwise might not, when Cassie eavesdrops on conversations which she is not supposed to hear. This is a clever piece of writing by Mildred Taylor, because it draws the reader into the story as a witness to incidents, just like the narrator, and allows us to understand the full impact of such things when they sometimes cause Cassie to become frightened and have nightmares about what she overhears.

Cassie is a bright, kind and caring person who has an independent mind. She has a strong sense of justice and a quick temper which, together with her courageous approach to unfairness, get her into trouble on a number of occasions. She refuses to accept a book at school when it becomes clear that it has been discarded by white students as being thought fit only for black children. She also shows enthusiasm for revenge against whites who have wronged black families; against T.J. for cheating Stacey out of his new coat and losing her mother her teaching job; and after her father is attacked and hurt. But, encouraged by her father, she learns that in her own best interests, and that of others, it is often wiser to react to events in a more thoughtful, planned and careful way. A good example of this is 'Miz' Lillian Jean's humiliating treatment of her in Chapter 5, and Cassie's solution (in Chapter 8) to dealing with this. She learns to use the same careful approach that Stacey uses when organising their revenge on the Jefferson Davis school bus.

Cassie's strong sense of justice sometimes causes her pain and suffering, as when Mr Barnett treats her differently to the white customers in his store. She cannot understand why he or Mr Simms treats her differently and it is only through such painful first-hand experiences that she learns about racism and intolerance. She feels betrayed and hurt when Big Ma fails to support her and it is only after her mother has explained the difficult situation Big Ma was in that Cassie finds herself able to forgive her.

By the end of the story Cassie and the reader have learned a lot about what it means to grow up in a prejudiced and intolerant environment for a black child in Mississippi in the 1930s. Cassie has also learned that her self-respect is more important than what other people think of her, but that standing up for principles always has a price. She has learnt that part of growing up is to do with learning to decide which issues are worth defending and that there are some ways of going about this which are more successful than others. She also comes to see that people sometimes have to take great risks to defend those things which are important to them.

Stacey

Stacey

Stacey, at 12 years of age, is the eldest of the Logan children and, especially as his father is away for so much of the year, feels at times a particularly sharp sense of responsibility because of this. We see this, for example, when he worries that the visit of the night men to the house and the threats of violence against the family are because of the wrecking of the school bus, which was his idea. His growing sense of adulthood leads him at first to resent the arrival of Mr Morrison, but this feeling does not last for long.

Unlike his younger sister, Cassie, he has a clear idea about how things work in the prejudiced and intolerant times in which they live. In his careful planning to wreck the school bus he understands the importance of trying to make it look like an accident and of why the children should behave in a way that will not draw suspicion to them. He also knows that protesting against injustice has to be done with care, and therefore sees why Big Ma has to make Cassie apologise to 'Miz' Lillian Jean, even though it is Cassie who is in the right.

Stacey's age puts him into the difficult period between being a child and a grown adult and this means that sometimes he is unsure of how he should behave towards others – Cassie has to remind him on one occasion that he is not her mother and that she will decide for herself what she does. Stacey's friendship with T.J. never really recovers from T.J.'s irresponsible and unkind treatment towards others, and weakens further after T.J. tricks him into parting with his new coat. His high standards of honour, however, will not allow him to reveal that it is actually T.J. who has been guilty of cheating at school, or to say anything which would get others into trouble following their fight. T.J.'s betrayal of the children's mother finally convinces Stacey that he must look elsewhere for his friends. Nonetheless, towards the end of the novel Stacey feels obliged to help the injured T.J. home late at night after he has been beaten, although he is careful to make sure that none of the family are discovered there when the night men arrive. Stacey's behaviour during this incident shows calmness and maturity and he ensures that a warning of what is happening gets to his father in good time.

He senses that the white Jeremy Simms would be a better friend than the black T.J., but is beginning to understand from what his father teaches him that relationships between black and white are unlikely to work.

T.J. Avery

T.J. is a tall, thin boy who is feared by his own younger brother, Claude, and disliked by the other children in the story. He is in the seventh grade at school, like Stacey, and is a character who sets much of the story's violent action into motion. He is a liar, a cheat, and a thief and although he uses his friendship with the Logan children to his own advantage, it is to them that he turns when he is in desperate need for help at the end of the novel. He is poorly disciplined at home – probably because his father is too ill to punish him – and has a weak character, which makes him easy prey for temptation. He is gullible and his need for attention results in him being easily tricked by the white Simms brothers into thinking that they are his friends, when in fact they regard him as a figure of fun to be used for their own amusement. T.J. is a strong contrast to the Logan children and his insecurity is the cause of much of his poor behaviour.

He is prepared to steal, as when he looks around Mrs Logan's room for the question papers and immediately lies about what he is doing. He also 'tells tales' about Mrs Logan and is the main cause of her being fired from her job.

T.J. is a character for whom, like Cassie, we might almost feel sorry, if we did not also feel that his misfortune is at least partly his own fault. Sadly, he is, as a black, at a severe disadvantage when eventually he ends up in a position where he will have to try to explain that his 'accomplices' in the robbery were white, and that it was they who committed the violence on Mr and Mrs Barnett.

When Cassie cries for T.J. and the land, she is crying for the waste of his talent and life, and the degradation of the human spirit.

Mr Morrison

Mr L.T. Morrison is an exceptionally tall and well-muscled man who has scars round his face and neck, as if caused by fire. His huge stature, together with his deep voice, the deep lifelines in his face and his 'grey splotched hair', give him a mysterious and impressive air. At their first meeting with him, the children regard him as a 'giant'. He is brought home by David Logan (Papa) to look after the family whilst he is away working, but Mr Morrison soon becomes a valued member of the family. He acts as the family's guardian angel, guiding Stacey into the correct behaviour after the fight and earning his respect by saying that he will not tell his mother about it because he knows that Stacey will decide to tell her himself. In many ways Mr Morrison takes David Logan's place whilst he is away.

Mr Morrison appreciates the warmth and love of the Logan home and we understand why this may mean so much to him when we learn about the violent death of his parents at the hands of the 'night men' and how his mother and father were a product of the 'breeding farms' of the slave trade. Mr Morrison is a quiet, calm and even-tempered man who nonetheless possesses great strength, which he uses when required.

He is, however, always careful not to behave in a way which will allow the local whites to persecute him, and a good example of this is his moving of Kaleb Wallace's truck. The Wallace family embody the brutal, physical side of racism and are quite prepared to maim or kill on the slightest pretext, or none at all. There is some satisfaction for the reader when they foolishly take on the strength of Mr Morrison.

Although he is a man of great physical strength, Mr Morrison knows that the battle against racial inequality and prejudice cannot be won by brute force alone. Mr Morrison is a source of foresight, good judgement and integrity in the novel, as shown when he prevents the hot-headed Hammer from attacking Charlie Simms.

It is, however, clear that Mr Morrison's dignity, strength of character and refusal to behave subserviently greatly irritates many of the local white bigots, like the Wallaces and Harlan Granger. It is to Mr Morrison that David Logan owes his life after they are attacked by the Wallaces, and it is Mr Morrison who inflicts such damage on two of the Wallace brothers and protects the Logan house every night by keeping watch for the night men.

Harlan Granger and Wade Jamison

These men represent the two opposing views of blacks taken by local white people.

Harlan Granger

Harlan Granger lives very much according to the values of the past and despises all blacks. He sees it as his personal crusade to buy back all the land which used to belong to his family before the Civil War and he resents the Logans because they are independent people who will not sell. Harlan Granger typifies the racist bigot. He believes the land should be his by right, a right that blacks do not have. It is therefore particularly galling to him that a black man legally holds land that used to belong to him. His racist attitude is shown when he visits the Logans and tries to persuade them to sell their land. When they refuse he at once resorts to threats.

He also resents the Logan's refusal to shop at the local Wallace store, from which he gets an income. He threatens his own farm workers with eviction and increases his share of their cotton crop when it seems as though the Logans are winning support from other families. Mostly, however, Harlan Granger resents any suggestion that blacks could in any way be the equal of whites and reacts violently to any such suggestion. It is clear that he is behind the sacking of Mary Logan and the bank manager's sudden calling in of their loan on the land. He is a man who holds a grudge for a long time; he still resents Mr Jamison because he sold some land to the Logans. At the end of the story he shows his indifference to the fate of all blacks by making it clear that he does not care what happens to T.J., just so long as nothing happens on his land which will cause him problems.

Wade Jamison

Mr Jamison is a white lawyer who recognises the injustices of the racial prejudice in the area. He is an enlightened man who represents a different set of values from the 'Old South' than does Harlan Granger. He does what he can to help blacks, and represents the changing attitudes of whites and the hope for a more tolerant society in the future. It seems possible that Jeremy Simms may grow up into a character like Wade Jamison.

Mr Jamison recognises the wrongs done to black people, but also that he is severely restricted in what he can do to help. He willingly gives genuine advice, and he takes a very dangerous step when he agrees to guarantee their debts, especially as it seems likely that he may lose a lot of money as a result. He is well-mannered, calm and has a mask-like face which gives away very little of what he is thinking. His actions give David Logan and his brother food for thought.

Mr Jamison's actions at the end of the story prevent the certain hanging of T.J. by the mob. He ignores the threats made to his life and the way many local whites regard him as a 'nigger lover' and tells the Logans that there are many whites who think as he does but that as yet they are too afraid to speak out. At the end of the story, he makes it clear that he knows what David Logan has done to save the situation and advises him to stay out of sight for a while. Whilst Harlan Granger does not care what happens to others and is concerned only about his own position, Mr Jamison risks his life for the principles of fairness and justice.

Christopher-John

Christopher-John is a naturally cheerful and happy seven-year-old child. He is short and 'round', and likes it when everyone is at ease with everyone else. He dislikes arguments and his sensitivity to the atmosphere between people makes him unhappy when arguments erupt. His nature is naturally sunny and we learn early on that he 'took little interest in troublesome things, preferring to remain on good terms with everyone'. He enjoys the good things in life, especially his food, and is thunderstruck when Stacey suggests that his plan to gain revenge on the school bus will involve him in missing a meal: he 'greatly questioned the wisdom of a plan so drastic that it could exclude lunch'. His dislike of arguments leads him to be a naturally obedient child who becomes unhappy when he follows his brother and sister to the Wallace store against their parents' instructions. He is also unhappy at taking T.J. home, because he knows that they should not be out alone so late at night. At the end of the story he refuses to leave the house to go and witness the fire.

Little Man

Little Man (Clayton Chester Logan) is a six-year-old who likes to keep himself spotlessly clean and neat. He is in the first grade at school as the story begins and is the one who is most hurt by the way the white children constantly torment and belittle blacks. He has a powerful sense of self-respect and shares the Logan family passion for justice and fairness. This is why he is reduced to tears when his clothes are dirtied once too often by the school bus and he complains bitterly to Big Ma. It also explains his strong reaction to the book he is given at school and the reason why he is prepared to be punished for refusing to take it rather than abandon his standards. Because of his strong feelings and his youth he does not understand the reason for Cassie's behaviour towards 'Miz' Lillian Jean, but by the end of the book he has come to understand more about the troubled relationships between black and white.

The Simms family

Jeremy Simms is a white boy who accompanies the other children to and from the crossroads on their walk to school each day, for which he is often ridiculed by the other white children at his school. Although he is laughed at by many of the other white children, Jeremy perhaps represents the hope for the future in being the only white child to treat the Logans as friends and equals. The Logan children only slowly come to understand how isolated Jeremy is from the other whites and how genuine he is in his friendship for them, especially Stacey. Stacey eventually comes to see that Jeremy would make an excellent friend, but is cautioned by his father that as both he and Jeremy grow up it is likely that such a friendship will break down. Jeremy and Stacey could be friends as children, but the adult world at that time would make such a friendship between adults of different colour extremely difficult. However, we see that Jeremy is sincere in his regard for the Logan children, as when he sticks up for Cassie in Strawberry, much to his own father's anger. Similarly, he is concerned for the children's welfare after the fire breaks out and brings presents for the family at Christmas. Jeremy is markedly different to the rest of his family.

Lillian Jean Simms is accidentally bumped by Cassie in the street in Strawberry and demands an apology. Although Cassie apologises, Lillian Jean is determined to humiliate her and is supported in this by her aggressive father. After humiliating Cassie, she fails completely to appreciate that Cassie's sudden friendship towards her is a ploy to get even. Eventually, after being beaten by Cassie in the forest, she becomes a little more subdued but still does not understand how offensive her behaviour has been or why Cassie has suddenly changed. Lillian Jean is an example of how unthinking racial prejudice and intolerance can be passed on by parents to their children, from one generation to another.

Melvin and R.W. Simms are the two idle brothers who have dropped out of school and spend their time hanging around the stores and getting into trouble. They befriend T.J. and use him for amusement by pretending to be his friends. R.W. is especially vicious, as when he hits Mr Wallace and his wife in the robbery of their store. Melvin and R.W. have no hesitation in beating T.J. and turning him in to protect themselves after the robbery. It seems clear that T.J. will hang for their crimes, but it is unlikely that they will be concerned about the life of a black.

Themes and images in
Roll of Thunder, Hear My Cry

Land ownership

Land ownership

Land and its ownership underlies much of what happens in the story. The history of black people in America dates from when they were taken from their own lands in Africa and sold into slavery. Ever since, black people have been dispossessed. Therefore, to own land signifies possession. It means independence and freedom. With the freeing of the slaves and the granting of the right to own property, it became possible for blacks to own land. The Logans own 200 acres of land outright and another 200 acres for which they have a mortgage. The importance to them, psychologically and financially, of owning their own land is stressed in almost every chapter and their struggle to retain it governs much of their working lives and often directly affects their behaviour.

Black people owning land in Mississippi is seen as provocative by most local whites. It increases the racists' hatred and provides them with the motivation for physical violence.

Big Ma takes Harlan Granger's threats to get the land back very seriously and she therefore arranges to transfer the ownership of her land to her two sons. Hammer is prepared to sacrifice all he owns to keep the land safe – even his beautiful car. Even though he is extremely proud of it, he takes the very down-to-earth view that a car cannot grow crops or become a home in which to raise a family.

David works away from home on the railway in order to increase the family's earnings. He teaches his children about the value of the land so that they will one day understand its importance. For the Logans, retaining the land is central to their lives. Their energies are directed towards ensuring they have the money to pay the mortgage. At first, Cassie cannot understand why the land is so important to the family, but by the end of the story this has changed and when she cries for T.J. and the land, she is also crying for freedom, dignity and equality.

Racism & Justice

Racism and justice

Cassie begins to understand that there is little justice for black people. Their school and its facilities are far inferior to those at Jefferson Davis school, where white children go. The white children's bus daily threatens their lives for the amusement of its occupants and even their school terms are shorter because it is recognised that the black children will be working the land during the spring and summer months. The black schoolteachers' pay is low and the working conditions inferior.

Cassie also learns, as does Stacey, that friendships between blacks and whites are not permitted and that whites have to be addressed by their full names – even the children have to be spoken to using titles like 'Miz', normally reserved for adults. Whites, on the other hand, speak to blacks in offensive terms, calling them 'boy', or 'nigger', freely. Blacks are expected to accept inferior treatment in shops, at the market and even when walking down the street. Even so, people like Harlan Granger and the Wallaces bitterly resent any small freedoms allowed to black people. In all their actions they show bitterness, whether by charging for goods not supplied, scheming to take land that is not theirs, or setting people on fire. For black people there is no recourse to justice for these events. To publicly complain would bring more violence and persecution on their heads, as Cassie learns in Strawberry when she dares to remind Mr Barnett that he has kept Cassie and Stacey waiting while he served white people before them.

Plantation owners pay their sharecroppers very little and even then they arrange matters so that they take most of what the sharecroppers grow and overcharge them for credit at the only stores they are allowed to use. Again, there is nothing the blacks can do about this.

Even the local sheriff calls a black woman witness a liar and makes no effort to see that T.J. gets proper treatment instead of being threatened with hanging by a mob, or that the whites who beat or kill blacks are brought to book.

In spite of this Stacey successfully takes revenge on the Jefferson Davis school bus, Cassie humiliates Lillian Jean, and the Logans manage to keep their land.

History

History

The historical background against which the events are set is very important, and the struggle against the history of slavery and the presence of racial prejudice and intolerance is central to the story. This is true both for the blacks and also for some of the whites. The history of the slave trade and its evil practices, such as the breeding farms, is explained to the children and Mr Morrison's childhood serves as a powerful example of this. The behaviour of black families in the novel is set in this context and influenced by the way they are treated by society. Through Big Ma and Mr Morrison, we learn how important it is for the black families to know about their history, to help them come to terms with the present.

Growing up

Growing up

The story is related in chronological order through about ten months in the life of the children from October 1933. During this brief period the children grow up considerably as a result of what happens around them and to them and learn important lessons about life.

Stacey has to come to terms with the actions of his friend, T.J., the 'intrusion' of Mr Morrison into the household, the brutal assault on his father, and the savage attack on T.J. His action in destroying the school bus, whilst successful, is dangerous. His pursuit of T.J. to the Wallaces is unwise, but understandable. When he gives his coat away he is responding to wounded vanity. Later, however, he shows greater maturity when he refuses to be fooled into giving T.J. the whistle from Jeremy. His punishment of T.J. after his mother loses her job is both calculating and effective. But despite everything, Stacey is still able to cry for his friend when it becomes obvious that T.J. has a very poor hold on life.

Cassie is more bewildered by the world she finds herself in; she cannot understand the injustices around her and does not recognise their dangers. She stands up against her teacher in support of Little Man but does not realise the danger of behaving like this when white people are involved. She comes close to disaster when she confronts the shopkeeper at Barnett's Mercantile, and immediately afterwards she falls foul of Mr Simms when she attempts to argue her rights. This is a low point for Cassie, but her revenge upon Lillian Jean is well-planned and executed. She shows a great deal of sensitivity, particularly in her response to the loneliness of Jeremy, for her mother after the dismissal from her job, and for T.J. when she cries for him at the end of the book.

■ Text commentary

Chapter 1

It is October 1933 in Mississippi and Little Man, Stacey, Christopher-John and Cassie Logan are on their way to school on the first day of the school year. Their friend T.J. tells the other children about the previous night's burning of the Berry's property by white men. The Jefferson Davis school bus for white children passes them by and covers Little Man in clouds of dust, dirtying his clean clothes. Jeremy, a local white boy, accompanies them on their walk as far as the crossroads. At school, the children are given old reading books to use and Little Man is furious when he sees that the books are old throwaways by white students and have now been reserved for 'nigras'. Both Little Man and Cassie are beaten for refusing to accept the books.

I tugged again at my collar and dragged my feet...

We learn a lot about each of the children in the first few pages of the novel.

Cassie

This is skilfully done by Mildred Taylor by having what they say to each other mixed with Cassie's thoughts. Cassie feels imprisoned by her clothes and it is clear that she normally does not wear shoes. She feels the restriction of attending school all the more when she thinks of all the other things she could be doing instead. Little Man is delighted with his neat and clean appearance. Stacey appears subdued, in contrast to Christopher-John, who is characteristically cheerful. Notice how well this device by the author allows you to quickly get to know something of the children, their standard of living, their relationships with each other and about their mother's teaching job at the school. It also allows Cassie to 'drift off' into her own thoughts, which – as she is the narrator of the story – we then 'overhear' and learn about the history of how the Logans got their land.

'Ah, man, don't look so down,' T.J. said cheerfully.

T.J. Avery

Stacey is subdued at the thought of spending all year being taught by his mother. When T.J. praises her teaching we see the author's ironic humour; Cassie observes to herself that her mother had been so successful with T.J. last year that he was 'returning for a second try'. We see this same humorous touch a little later on, where it is also used to

25

emphasise how young Little Man is when he innocently asks T.J. what death looks like, completely ruining the atmosphere of suspense which T.J. was trying to build up.

The prospect of Stacey being in his mother's class immediately suggests for T.J. the possibility of passing her examinations by cheating. This dishonest and 'street-wise' attitude is an important feature of T.J.'s character which is cleverly introduced here the first time we meet him.

'Burning? What burning?'

Why do you think the Logan children's mother kept this news from them?

T.J. Avery

We see that T.J. likes to be involved in matters which are probably too old for him. Cassie has already told her mother about T.J.'s visits to a disreputable local store, for which he has got his own brother Claude into trouble rather than take the blame himself. Look at the way our negative view of T.J. is cleverly and quickly generated by what he says, his attitude to others and the kinds of values he has, together with the Logan children's reactions towards him. This is a much more subtle, but effective, technique than simply telling us that he is a person of poor character, and is a skilful piece of writing by the author.

Mildred Taylor is careful not to produce stereotype characters, and we see in the story admirable and flawed characters, both black and white. T.J. is 'balanced', in this respect, by Jeremy Simms, just as Harlan Granger is balanced by Mr Jamison. Other balances also appear and you should be on the lookout for them in this carefully crafted novel.

... spewing clouds of red dust like a huge yellow dragon breathing fire.

The bus is an uncontrollable, fierce monster from which there is little chance

Racism & Justice

to escape and is a symbol of the cruel and racist way many local whites behave towards blacks. More evidence of this appears in Chapter 3, when the behaviour of the bus and the way it is described as 'a living thing, plaguing and defeating us at every turn' emphasise it as a symbol for the real enemy in their lives. Do you think the bus driver is deliberately trying to hit the children? Would he or his employers be upset, do you suppose, if one of them was killed 'accidentally'? Consider these questions again when you come across the other occasions when the children are tormented by the bus and its 'laughing white faces'.

There was an awkward silence.

Jeremy Simms is a young white boy who, unlike many adults, is happy to offer

Growing up

friendship for its own sake, irrespective of the colour of the skin of others. His friendship is not always well-received by the Logan children, or by his own family and other white children. Jeremy's behaviour emphasises that there is hope for the future between black and white, and that this hope lies in the children. David Logan – the children's father – offers Stacey advice about this later, in Chapter 7.

Great Faith School

The description of the school and its setting tells us much about the life of the

Racism & Justice

black community. It is deprived and tumble-down and in many senses has its 'back to the wall'. Even the amount of education which black children get is less than whites, and the drop-out rate is very high. Notice that after the first day many of the clothes which the children wear will be put away. Why is this?

The name of Great Faith School is significant, as is its location next to the community church. This represents the hope for the future for black families. Everything about the school is in contrast to the luxuriously equipped Jefferson Davis School for whites, with its flag of Mississippi, emblazoned with the Confederate emblem, deliberately flying above the American flag in the centre of its expansive front lawn.

Girls with blond braids and boys with blue eyes stared up at me.

Why is Cassie's first view of inside her book so revealing for us? Notice that

Growing up

it does not at first produce any impact on Cassie and think about what this tells you regarding her present acceptance of the world the way it is. So why is her younger brother's reaction so much more extreme? Notice that once Little Man has taken a stand Cassie sides with him. This is not simply loyalty to her brother – as she tries to explain to Miss Crocker. But like many other adults, both black and white, Miss Crocker looked at life around her but 'understood nothing' of what it meant.

'Biting the hand that feeds you. That's what you're doing, Mary Logan, …'

History

Mary Logan understands why the books have caused a problem and, although she is careful not to undermine the authority of Daisy Crocker, she makes it clear that she has no intention of encouraging her children to accept the unfairness of the world the way it is. Like her children, Mary Logan refuses to be defined by what others think, and this is why she covers the offensive pages in the books. For the same reason she later refuses to abide by what the textbooks say about the history of slavery when she knows it to be a distortion, even though her stand on this issue costs her dearly.

Cassie overhears the conversation between her mother and Miss Crocker. This device is used several times in the book to allow us to 'overhear' things which we are not told directly. This technique cleverly draws the reader into the story by allowing them to 'know' things which some of the characters do not.

Mama's origins outside the county make her something of an 'outsider', even after 14 years. This tells us a lot about how the more 'traditional' thinkers like Miss Crocker regard anything which disturbs their lives. It also helps to explain why entrenched attitudes are so hard to change in such communities, even today.

Chapter 2

The children's father returns home one Saturday from working away, but says he can stay only until Sunday evening, when he must board the train back again. He has brought home Mr L.T. Morrison, who is to stay a while with the family. During a conversation between the Avery and Lanier families after church on Sunday, we learn more about the actions of some white men who are terrorising and murdering black families.

'Papa, what you doing home?'

Welcome though their father's return is, it is clear that he is not expected. What hints are we given in this chapter that he may have returned home because all is not well? Whilst Chapter 1 concentrated on the children's view of their lives, Chapter 2 tells us something about how the adults in the Logan family see the world around them.

Racism & Justice

...the most formidable-looking being we had ever encountered...

Notice the way in which Mr Morrison is described – he is a 'tree', towering over their father's six feet two inches, with a 'massive body', scarred skin 'as if by fire', with deep lifelines in his face and 'clear and penetrating' eyes. His stature is that of some god-like 'giant' whose voice is 'like the roll of low thunder'. His attributes make him immune to the physical threats by which the local whites terrorise the black community. The most significant thing the children learn from him is that in spite of his immensely powerful presence, he is a softly-spoken, peaceable man who avoids physical violence wherever possible. It is clear that he was blamed for the fight which got him sacked from his job because he was black, not because he was in the wrong.

Its walls were made of smooth oak...

The Logan house has a strong sense of family history, of the family's traditions and its ancestors, and has a feeling of permanence and continuity. It is a stable, established, solid home. Notice the number of items which are of oak or walnut – which are slow-growing and long-lived trees. The living strength and permanence of timber and trees (like those planted by Big Ma and Grandpa Logan) are a symbol of the strength which the black community draws from its history, tradition and inheritance, and the 'roots' which have been put down in their land.

History

'Sayin' they'd do it again if some uppity nigger get out of line.'

The whites in the story always like to have some excuse – however flimsy – for their persecution of blacks. Mr Morrison was accused of starting the fight and was sacked. What was John Henry Berry supposed to have done? You are given considerable cause to suppose that he was in fact innocent of doing anything wrong. It is clear that some whites regularly go around terrorising and killing blacks and that very little is done about this by the rest of the white community, as their actions are well known by everyone. If some whites feel so secure about their behaviour that they can brag publicly that they will do the same again, why is it that they need the pretence of some excuse? What does this tell you about how they regard the justification for their own behaviour?

Racism & Justice

'In this family, we don't shop at the Wallace store.'

At first sight, Papa's statement seems strange and meaningless. What is it that tells us that he has touched on a dangerous topic? (Look at the reactions of the other adults). Papa gives the children a reason for avoiding the Wallace store but later, in Chapter 4, we learn that there is more to it than this. Like their mother, Papa tells the children enough to keep them safe and out of trouble, and advises them about their behaviour, but does not reveal all his worries and thoughts. We are aware of this on a number of occasions when the adults in the family talk but the children are sent to bed. Occasionally the children overhear snippets of conversation which frighten them. Do you think the children would be more frightened, or less frightened, if their parents told them all their worries? Is this something which modern parents also do today where their children are concerned?

Mr Logan & Uncle Hammer

Chapter 3

It is the end of October and heavy rains have come. The Jefferson Davis school bus continues to deliberately splash the children with mud. Stacey plans to prevent the bus from bothering the children for a while by digging large holes in the road. They watch at the end of the day as the bus crashes into their trap and the white students have to walk home through the pouring rain. News of the wrecked bus causes great amusement in the Logan house that evening. Mr Avery calls and interrupts their evening to warn the family that the night riders are out again. The children are sent to bed but Cassie, whilst pretending to be asleep, sees Big Ma come into her bedroom and collect a rifle from under her bed. Awakening in the night, Cassie goes outside in search of Big Ma. She sees several cars approach through the rain and stop in the driveway. The cars depart after the men inside them seem to decide this is not the house they are looking for.

'Nigger! Nigger! Mud eater!'

The children's carefully calculated revenge against the bus contains a lesson

about how blacks must deal with white persecution. Stacey knows that it is important to be sure that they are not suspected and that the crash be made to look like an accident. He knows that none of them must speak of the plan either before or afterwards and, significantly, he excludes the loud-mouthed T.J. from everything to do with the incident. He will not even tell his own brothers and sister what his plan is beforehand. Later on we see

Stacey

Cassie successfully adopt the same approach to dealing with 'Miz' Lillian Jean. Papa also follows this method when dealing with the mob by setting the fire at the end of the novel. Contrast this with the bragging behaviour of the whites who persecute local families. Dealing successfully with bullying and intolerance is a matter of actions speaking louder than words, and by the end of the novel Cassie has learnt that there are some things, like the burning of the cotton, which are never to be spoken of, not even within the family, and that the sweetest revenge is the most well concealed.

Jeremy never rides the bus

Every time Jeremy tries to make friends with the children he is rebuffed or, as here, rejected outright. In the face of this, why do you think he keeps trying to be friendly and why does he never go on the bus? Why does he want to be friends with Stacey when he could presumably have plenty of white friends? These are not easy questions to answer, given the sort of background and family Jeremy comes from. Compare Jeremy's behaviour with that of Mr Jamison for a possible clue to the way he treats the Logans. Both are examples of admirable white characters who are abused by other whites for daring to step outside accepted patterns of bigoted behaviour.

Growing up

The destruction of the bus

Notice how, in keeping with the way it has been described so far, the destruction of the bus appears as the death of some living creature which 'sputtered a last murmuring protest' before dying 'like a lopsided billy goat on its knees'. Notice also that although the bus is thoroughly wrecked, the children have gained victory without hurting anyone.

Racism & Justice

Then all of us began to laugh...

We are not told whether the rest of the family know the truth about the crashing of the bus, but the incident causes much amusement in the Logan household and we may wonder how much they suspect. This is a nice touch by Mildred Taylor, who seems to have left us to wonder for ourselves how much is known but unspoken – especially as the adults never question the children in any depth about their persistent amusement following the crash.

Mr Avery calls with news about the night men

As soon as Mama suspects what Mr Avery has called about she packs the children off to bed, but they sneak back to overhear him say that the night men ride whenever they feel that the blacks are stepping out of their place. Notice how the mention of Mr Grimes, the appropriately named school bus driver, causes Stacey to assume that it is the wrecking of the bus which has prompted events. Notice too how his guilt about this causes him to snap at the others,

Racism & Justice

although his growing sense of adult responsibility also causes him to offer to help deal with the threat. Later, we learn from T.J. that Stacey appears to have worried for nothing, but so unreliable is T.J. that we are never fully sure about the truth. There are several places in the novel where this device is used to leave the reader in suspense about what is really happening. This technique contrasts cleverly with the way the story is recounted via Cassie to lead us to think we are being told everything.

The night men call

In a similar way Mildred Taylor skilfully controls the tension when, later that

Cassie

night, Cassie wakens to find the watching Big Ma and her rifle gone. Hearing a noise on the porch and assuming it to be her brothers, she goes out and is terrified when the dog leaps on her, affectionately licking her face. Swiftly following her relief comes terror as she sees the night men approaching. Notice how their presence is more terrifying because they do not actually do anything – it is the threat of what they might have done which is so frightening. The sight of the protective Mr Morrison hiding in the darkness further heightens the tension, producing uncontrollable trembling in Cassie.

The tradition of story telling as seen in *Roll Of Thunder*

Mildred Taylor often recalled how she was entranced as a child, listening to relatives and neighbours tell stories about the past. This oral tradition of **story telling** runs through *Roll Of Thunder*, not just in the way Big Ma or Mr Morrison recall their ancestors and the heritage of the past to Cassie and the other children, but also in the general structure of the novel, with its emphasis on recounting events through the eyes of Cassie as a **narrator** and on keeping them strictly in **chronological order** (the order in which they happened). We can also see echoes of the author's own past in many of the novel's characters – look at the 'Author's Note' at the start of the novel for evidence. In this sense, much of the novel is autobiographical.

As is common in the black cultural tradition of learning about history through story telling, the younger characters in *Roll Of Thunder* have the dark realities of racism explained to them and the tale features several characters who are strong role models of courage. The coming together of the black community in its fight against white injustice is the rising storm of the 'roll of thunder' in the title. Big Ma and Mr Morrison are kindly sharers of wisdom as well as comforting and protecting figures and act as living connections with black history. These characters, ideas and the story itself are further developed in Mildred Taylor's next novel in the series, *Let The Circle Be Unbroken*.

Self-test (Questions) Chapters 1–3

Uncover the plot

Delete two of the three alternatives given, to find the correct plot. Beware possible misconceptions and muddles.

Cassie Logan and her cousins/brothers/neighbours Little Man, Stacey and Christopher-John live in Alabama/Louisiana/Mississippi with their mother and their housekeeper/grandmother/cook Big Ma. Their father is presently away in Carolina/Louisiana/Memphis laying railroad track.

On their way to school one morning in October 1933 the children meet T.J. Avery and a white boy, Jeremy Simms, who walks part of the way with them on their way to school. A teacher, Miss Lanier/Davis/Crocker, gives out some books. Berry/Little Man/T.J. and Cassie/Mary Lou/Gracey are beaten when they refuse to accept them because they have been bought/used/discarded by white children.

Shortly afterwards, Cassie and her brothers are helping their mother/Big Ma/Mr Morrison to pick cotton when they see their father and a friend approaching. Mr Crocker/Morrison/Wallace is going to stay a while; he lost his job with the railroad because he was drunk/in a fight/always late. Some other men who were involved did not get fired because they were white/good workers/well behaved. At church the next day the family learn of the murder of Mr Berry/Mr Lanier/Mr Avery. It is suspected that he was killed by local thieves/white men/down-and-outs.

One winter's day on the way to school the children are forced into the slimy gully/wet forest/schoolyard by the passing school bus. Stacey/Little Man/Cassie plans revenge. The children secretly bury a log/dig a hole/pile up rocks in the road. The bus driver does not sense the danger and the bus crashes/stops/is covered in mud. It seems as though the wrecking/stopping/dirtying of the bus may have provoked the night riders into action. The children worry that the riders are coming after their parents/Mr Morrison/them. During the night, men on horses/on foot/in cars arrive at the house, but go away again.

Who? What? Why? When? Where? How?

1 Why, in the Spring of 1931, did Papa set out looking for work on the railroad?
2 Who hates shoes and prefers their freedom-loving feet to feel the warm earth?
3 In which two years did the children's grandfather buy 200 acres of Granger land?
4 On whose land did the Avery family live as sharecroppers?
5 Why do Cassie, Little Man and Stacey dislike T.J.?
6 What are the first hints in this chapter that there may be trouble ahead?
7 Of what material were the walls of Mama and Papa's room made?
8 What does Papa mean when he threatens the children that he will 'wear y'all out'?
9 Where did 'the burnings' take place?
10 Why does Stacey not pick cotton like the other children?
11 Who never rides the school bus, no matter how bad the weather?
12 Who suggests that the children do not wait in the forest for the bus, but return to the road?
13 What does Mama wear every day on her feet to protect them from the mud and rain?
14 Why does Mama send the children to bed when the visitor arrives?
15 Why is Stacey especially upset at the news about the night riders?

Character Clues

1 Who is more afraid of T.J. than of their own mother?
2 Who says: 'What does death look like?'
3 Who does Miss Crocker think is 'Biting the hand that feeds you'?
4 Who refused to pick up a book?
5 Who 'had looked at the page and had understood nothing'?
6 Which frail sickly man has a hacking cough?
7 What, according to Mama, do some of the older children do after school at the Wallace store?
8 Why did the Laniers and the Averys look 'uneasily about them'?
9 Who has 'a deep, quiet voice like the low roll of thunder'?
10 Who always meant what they said?
11 Who shout 'Nigger! Nigger! Mud eater!'?
12 Whose body is racked with uncontrollable trembling?
13 Why is Jeremy Simms always 'hanging round' the children?
14 Whose first name is Harlan?

Self-test (Answers) Chapters 1–3

Uncover the plot

Cassie Logan and her brothers Little Man, Stacey and Christopher-John live in Mississippi with their mother and their grandmother Big Ma. Their father is presently away in Louisiana laying railroad track.

On their way to school one morning in October 1933 the children meet T.J. Avery and a white boy, Jeremy Simms, who walks part of the way with them on their way to school. A teacher, Miss Crocker, gives out some books. Little Man and Cassie are beaten when they refuse to accept them because they have been discarded by white children.

Shortly afterwards, Cassie and her brothers are helping Big Ma to pick cotton when they see their father and a friend approaching. Mr Morrison is going to stay a while; he lost his job with the railroad because he was in a fight. Some other men who were involved did not get fired because they were white. At church the next day the family learn of the murder of Mr Berry. It is suspected that he was killed by local white men.

One winter's day on the way to school the children are forced into the slimy gully by the passing school bus. Stacey plans revenge. The children secretly dig a hole in the road. The bus driver does not sense the danger and the bus crashes. It seems as though the wrecking of the bus may have provoked the night riders into action. The children worry that the riders are coming after them. During the night, men in cars arrive at the house, but go away again.

Who? What? Why? When? Where? How?

1 Because the price of cotton dropped
2 Cassie
3 1887 and 1918
4 On Granger land
5 Because he got his brother punished for something which he himself did wrong
6 Papa has come home suddenly; Papa has brought Mr Morrison to stay with the family whilst he returns to working away from home
7 Smooth oak
8 That he will beat them with a switch (a flexible twig or cane)
9 Over by Smellings Creek
10 He is now too heavy to climb the poles
11 Jeremy Simms
12 T.J.
13 Papa's old field shoes
14 She thinks she has brought news about the night riders which could frighten the children
15 It was his idea to wreck the bus; so he thinks the riders are out, and the family at risk, because of him

Character Clues

1 T.J.'s brother, Claude
2 Little Man
3 Mary Logan
4 Little Man
5 Miss Crocker, when she was shown the chart inside the cover
6 T.J.'s father
7 Dance, buy bootleg liquor and smoke cigarettes
8 The conversation makes them uncomfortable, because they shop at the Wallace store
9 Mr Morrison
10 Papa
11 The white children on the school bus
12 Cassie
13 He says it is because he likes them
14 Mr Granger

34

Chapter 4

Big Ma and Mama are worried that the children seem not to be themselves recently. The children are reassured to learn that the night men were not out because of what happened to the bus. Stacey is beaten at school by Mama for cheating in a test, although it is T.J. who is really responsible. Mr Morrison stops a fight between the two boys at the Wallaces' store. We learn about how the Logans came to own their land. The children are taken to visit Mr Berry, who is badly disfigured from the burning.

'Somethin' the matter with that child, Mary.'

The technique which we saw used at the end of the last chapter is here seen

again, but cleverly reversed. Because we and the children overheard the adults' conversation, we know about the children's fear of the night men. But the adults do not know that the children overheard, so now we know something which the adults do not. Notice how this conspiratorial tone is maintained when Cassie overhears Big Ma and Mama discussing how worried they are about her. But why does Cassie not tell her mother what is worrying her? What would telling her mother about her worries also mean that she had to tell her about? (T.J. unwittingly solves the problem in what he shortly tells the children.)

T.J. has a system for getting out of work

The 'system' T.J. talks about is, typically for him, one which involves

dishonesty. So we are not surprised when he adopts the same approach to passing his school tests. In telling what he knows about the night men, T.J. speaks the truth when he says that these are things which he should not know about. Look carefully at his attitude when describing what happened to Mr Tatum – this tells us how far from being mature, sensitive and grown up T.J. is. Think about what happens to T.J. at the end of the book and how he might have felt if the Logan children adopted the same attitude towards him as he always shows towards the suffering of other people. So why do you suppose T.J. behaves in this foolish and immature way? Think of what he is always trying to get from the other children (hint: they have become wise to what he wants and this chapter shows examples of how they try to avoid giving it to him).

A testing time

It seems possible that T.J. stole the test answers from Mama's room, as he has provided himself with a sheet of notes. In any event, Stacey's ripping them up does not stop T.J. making another set and, worse still, deliberately

Stacey

allowing Stacey to take the blame for him using them in the examination. On which other character has T.J. played this kind of trick? (Hint: he was more afraid of T.J. than his own mother.). In contrast to the way T.J. behaves, Stacey refuses to incriminate anyone else and takes the full blame himself. This includes a public whipping from his own mother in front of the class. Stacey's mother is here in the same position as Big Ma is in later in the novel, when Cassie is bullied in Strawberry. Both these events, like those which ultimately befall T.J., show how it is sometimes the case that being in the right is less important than how things are made to appear to others. Of which of the following events is this also true: Mr Morrison's fight and sacking, Mama's sacking, the burning of Mr Berry, the tarring and feathering of Mr Tatum? Consider how far this is also true for other racist incidents in the novel.

Stacey's determination to punish T.J. is strong enough for him to disobey his father and follow T.J. to the Wallace store, where the Wallaces laugh at 'all the little niggers' who have come to dance. Notice how, even during the fight, T.J.'s mean and underhand attitude is shown – he can gain the advantage only by pretending to be more hurt than he is.

The giant arrives

Mr Morrison intervenes to stop the fight. Notice how, when he passes the Wallace brothers, he 'looked through them as though they were not there'. This is both a measure of his attitude towards them and a skilful indication of the emptiness and worthlessness of their characters – they are vacant, idle people of no substance.

Stacey recognises that he owes it to his mother to tell her the truth

Big Ma & Mrs Logan

Stacey becomes much closer to Mr Morrison after he makes it plain that he will not be reporting the matter of the fight to Mama, because Stacey himself will. As this is precisely the point Stacey was defending at school – that T.J. should have had the character to admit his own errors but that others should not do it for him – so we should not be surprised that Stacey does finally own up about the fight to his mother. Again, he does so without implicating anyone else. How would T.J. have dealt with the same situation? How does the immediate reaction of Stacey's mother – compared to what the children were expecting – tell you that she recognises this increased maturity in her son?

Big Ma tells Cassie about the land

Big Ma tells Cassie about the strong sense of unity which she feels exists between her and the land. Her history, her memories of loved ones, her past

Land ownership

losses and her grief are all evoked by the land. This long section, carefully written as a conversation, is more of a look into Big Ma's history and her mind than a real chat between her and Cassie. It is also a very skilful way of telling the reader much of what they need to know to really understand the significance of many events in the story. We sense that Big Ma's memories draw her very strongly. She and the land are almost of one spirit, having grown old together through their various trials and tribulations. Significantly, the land means almost nothing in itself for Harlan Granger, who has more land already than he knows what to do with.

Telling Cassie about people and incidents from the past keeps them alive for Big Ma. The importance of this tradition of story telling, and the way it preserves a cultural history for the black community as a whole, is an idea which runs through the novel.

The children are taken to visit Mr Berry

The children are shown first-hand what some whites are prepared to do to blacks, and understand how such enemies are dangerous.

Growing up

More than any whipping or scolding, this explains to the children why they should not visit the Wallace store. Why, during their visit, do you think Mrs Berry is so cheerful? Is she simply glad to see visitors, or is her pleasant manner used to deliberately conceal something else? You are not told where Mrs Berry's own injuries came from, but can you guess? How strong the rule of law and order is can be seen from the way the Wallaces openly laugh about disfiguring Mr Berry, and indicates how carefully blacks must behave to protect themselves from similar treatment.

Mama begins to organise a boycott of the Wallace store

Following their visit to the Berrys, the children witness the character and

Big Ma & Mrs Logan

courage of their mother as she tries to persuade other families not to shop at the Wallace store. The growing strength of the anger of local families is shown by the fact that even after what happened to Mr Berry, some families are prepared to consider siding with Mama. But notice that everyone is careful to avoid talking openly about the Wallaces' actions, because that is not wise – 'There were too many ears that listened for others besides themselves, and too many tongues that wagged to those they shouldn't.' (Which character does this remind you of?)

The importance of the Logans' land is again emphasised; it is this which means that they do not have to 'cowtail', or defer, to white landowners, unlike many other families.

How the Logans got their land, following Reconstruction

In America after the Civil War (1861-1865) came a period known as Reconstruction (1865-1877). During Reconstruction the economy was still in ruins and times were hard for everyone, even the newly-freed slaves.

Mr Hollenbeck sold two hundred acres of land to Big Ma's husband, Paul Edward Logan, in 1887. Mr Hollenbeck was a **Yankee** (a Northerner) who bought two thousand acres of land during Reconstruction from the Grangers (Southerners, on the side of the **Confederates** during the Civil War). After the Civil War the Grangers' Confederate money was not worth anything and their property had been ransacked by soldiers of both sides, so they were desperate to sell some land in order to pay their taxes and rebuild the rest of it.

Harlan Granger's father, Filmore, was too mean to buy back the land, even though Mr Hollenbeck offered him the whole two thousand acres back for less than it was actually worth. So Mr Hollenbeck sold half of the land in several small pieces to local farmers – including that bought by Paul Edward Logan – and the other one thousand acres to Mr Jamison's father, Charles. It was Charles Jamison's son, Wade, who sold Paul Edward Logan a further two hundred acres and the rest to Harlan Granger, who bought out the other small farms at the same time. Granger had by then got back all the original two thousand acres except the two hundred owned by Paul Edward Logan, who refused to sell. Granger was determined to have everything back the way it was before the war and therefore still held a grudge against Wade Jamison for selling land to Paul Edward Logan in the first place. Paul Edward Logan therefore owned two hundred acres outright (which he bought from Mr Hollenbeck) and was paying for the other two hundred he bought from Mr Jamison through a mortgage (a loan from the bank).

Chapter 5

Stacey, Cassie and T.J. are taken to the market at Strawberry by Big Ma, where she sells some milk and eggs. Afterwards Big Ma goes to visit Mr Jamison, the attorney, and whilst she is gone the children go into Barnett Mercantile store where T.J. admires a pearl-handled handgun which is on display. T.J. gives Mr Barnett the list of items which Big Ma intended to buy and Cassie becomes annoyed at the way Mr Barnett keeps interrupting serving them to deal with other customers. When Cassie complains to Mr Barnett there is an argument and he becomes angry and tells them to leave. Once outside Cassie accidentally bumps into Lillian Jean Simms and is humiliated when Mr Simms and Big Ma make her apologise in a degrading way.

Off to Strawberry, at three-thirty in the morning

The twenty-two miles to Strawberry is a long trip by wagon and although

Stacey has been allowed to go before, it is clear that Cassie is being taken only because Big Ma has promised Mr Avery to take T.J., whom she obviously does not like very much. Cassie cannot see why Big Ma parks her wagon so far away from the best spot on the field. By now, you should be able to see why Big Ma's comment; 'Them's white folks' wagons', explains everything. In keeping with the way suspense is used to maintain interest throughout the novel, notice how the author does not tell the reader why Big Ma is visiting Wade Jamison. In fact the reader has to work this out alone (look at what happens in the second half of Chapter 7). Big Ma finds T.J.'s constant chattering tiresome, and later on tells him to be quiet on the journey home, and Cassie has suspected that this is why she has been allowed along. But it is not T.J. that Big Ma warns about not wanting any trouble. Following such strong warnings, why do things go so badly wrong for Cassie later that day?

Barnett Mercantile store – and a pearl-handled gun

Against his better judgement, Stacey leaves the wagon after being persuaded

by T.J., followed by a reluctant Cassie. How likely is it that Cassie or Stacey would have left the wagon of their own accord? What sort of an influence on others is T.J.? Cassie is at a loss to understand why T.J. admires the gun so much – in her innocence she cannot fathom what use it would be. But Stacey backs away nervously, knowing that the store is a hostile place for them. What is it that T.J. thinks the gun will give him that he does not already have?

Snakes

Cassie remarks that the gun would not even be good enough to 'hardly kill

a rattlesnake'. Not for the first time, T.J. speaks truer than he perhaps knows when he answers that 'there's other things a body need protectin' from more than a rattlesnake'. Although T.J. has in mind his own notion of what these 'other things' are, it seems clear that his thinking does not include the idea that people need 'protecting' in another sense – the love and protection of a family and strong moral values might, for example, have prevented T.J. ending up where he eventually does. Notice how the references to violence and to the snake – vermin fit only to be shot – echo across the next page or so: the children wait near a man 'measuring nails onto a scale'; Mr Barnett 'recoiled' (a word also used to describe a gun's action) 'as if I had struck him'; Cassie 'hissed' at him; Stacey's 'dark eyes flashed malevolently'; and Cassie 'whipped' her hand from his.

Why does T.J. want the gun?

T.J. Avery

T.J.'s longing for respect and attention mistakenly leads him to imagine that these can be gained by owning a gun which is clearly designed not for hunting food, but for killing people. Which other characters is T.J., perhaps unconsciously, copying here – who else has this kind of attitude to others? Read carefully the conversation between Cassie and her mother near the start of Chapter 6 for a clearer understanding of the important point being made here.

'I ain't nobody's little nigger!'

Cassie

Cassie is furious at the way Mr Barnett is treating them. But the older Stacey and T.J. do not protest at all, because they have learned something that Cassie is only now beginning to fully realise. When she protests to Stacey that Mr Barnett was in the wrong, he replies; 'I know it and you know it, but he don't know it, and that's where the trouble is'. Which other young member of the Logan family have we seen already start to learn this painful lesson? Find the description of Cassie's behaviour when alone after leaving the store and notice how it emphasises her youthful impetuosity.

Cassie walks into trouble

Racism & Justice

Because she is still preoccupied with her recent run-in with Mr Barnett, Cassie does not see Lillian Jean and accidentally walks into her. Although she apologises, Lillian Jean demands a humiliating apology from Cassie by saying she should walk in the dirty road. For the second time that day Cassie is insulted, when Lillian Jean contrasts her 'nasty little self' with 'decent white folks'. The fact that Lillian Jean feels that she has some kind of natural right to treat Cassie this way tells us a lot about how many white children were raised and the values their parents taught them. Remember that in Chapter 1 she has already bragged that Jeremy's bruises were the result of his friendship with blacks.

Notice how Jeremy tries to defend Cassie both to his sister and his father. We can see why Mr Simms' behaviour would frighten Cassie, but why is Jeremy afraid? Mr Simms, backed by his family and other townsfolk, bullies Cassie and Big Ma – who Mr Simms insultingly refers to as 'aunty' – into a humiliating apology. Only later does Cassie come to understand how little choice in the matter Big Ma had. Once she is away from her home, Big Ma knows how exposed she is. Like the incident in the Barnett store, Cassie is angered by the way she has been treated, but more by what she sees as betrayal and a deliberate lack of support from her own family. This is why the day has been 'cruel' to her.

Chapter 6

On their return home from the market at Strawberry, the children find that Uncle Hammer has come to visit and has brought his new Packard car, which is the same type as that owned by Mr Granger. When Uncle Hammer learns of Cassie's ordeal in Strawberry he becomes angry and drives off in his car to go and see Mr Simms. As Uncle Hammer leaves, Mr Morrison leaps into the car. Later that evening, Mama explains to Cassie why Mr Simms and Big Ma behaved the way they did. At breakfast the next day Uncle Hammer and Mr Morrison are home unscathed. Uncle Hammer gives Stacey a new coat, which is mocked by T.J. when the family go to church together. On the way home Uncle Hammer's car is mistaken for that of Mr Granger when the Wallace family stop to let him across a bridge first.

Hammer by name, hammer by nature

Stacey explains why Big Ma had no real choice in Strawberry, but is Cassie

also right in saying that her father would not have made her apologise? Your conclusion will depend on your assessment of David Logan's character. For Cassie it is a matter of either being on her side of things or not, and we now meet Uncle Hammer, who is somewhat like-minded to Cassie. What important contrast with the children's father is revealed by the way Mildred Taylor introduces us to this character? (Look especially at the description of his eyes.)

What does Uncle Hammer's dress and the fact that he has bought a car like Harlan Granger's, say about his character (apart from that he has money)? Big Ma's reaction contains a clue here. Big Ma knows her son's character well, and tries several times to prevent him hearing about what has happened in Strawberry. What clue in Mama's behaviour tells you that Big Ma has not told her either? (Hint: getting supper.)

'I ain't gotta use David's gun... I got my own.'

When Hammer hears about what happened in Strawberry, why does Mrs Logan immediately send Stacey for Mr Morrison? Which other character wants their own gun, and do these two people have anything in common? Notice how Christopher-John adopts the same attitude towards instant revenge as Cassie and Uncle Hammer, but that other members of the family, notably Stacey, do not. What character trait does Mr Morrison have which will be essential in successfully dealing with this situation?

The way things are

Mrs Logan explains to Cassie why things are the way they are, and why Big

Ma had little option in Strawberry but to behave the way she did. Her mother also explains something even more important in response to Cassie's; 'White ain't nothin'!' and she begins to learn why it is that some people – both white and black – need to feel superior, because they have so little else. Mrs Logan's account of why Mr Simms thinks the way he does is central to the novel and you should study it carefully.

Growing up

About slavery, the American War of Independence and the American Civil War

Between the sixteenth and nineteenth centuries, millions of men, women and children were transported by ship from West Africa, where they were exchanged for goods, to America. In the ships they were tightly packed together under inhuman conditions and many died on the journey. On arrival in America the survivors were used as **slaves**, mostly in the **Southern states**. They were treated more like animals than people, with men being sold for their strength whilst the younger women were treated as 'breeding stock'. Families were separated and many children never saw their parents again. Most slaves then worked under cruel and hard conditions in the cotton, sugar or tobacco **plantations** from dawn until dusk – even the children too if they were over five years old. The plantations were owned by whites who, as their owners, had complete control over the lives of the slaves and could mistreat them, or buy and sell them, as they saw fit. If a slave attacked a white person, or stole from them, they were often killed. Some slaves were treated less severely by their masters, but this was very rare.

Until 1776 the American colonies belonged to Britain, but the settlers wanted to be independent. Their **Declaration of Independence** in 1776 was only accepted after the bloody five-year War of Independence with Britain. George Washington became the first President of The Union (now called The United States). Following this the **Northern states** banned slavery because they said all men were created equal. This was not popular in the Southern states where, even though slavery was declared illegal in 1807 and banned in 1883, it continued. Many slaves ran away to the Northern States, often helped by sympathetic Southern whites. This disagreement between North and South was one of the things that led to the **American Civil War**.

When Abraham Lincoln became President of The Union in 1861 he was not well liked in the South because of his very outspoken condemnation of slavery. Seven states broke away from The Union and called themselves The Confederate States of America. When Lincoln called out the troops after they attacked a government fort, four more states broke away and the four-year-long Civil War began between the North (**Yankees**) and the South (**Confederates**). The Union, in the North, had far more people, whilst a quarter of the much smaller South's population was comprised of slaves. But the Southerners were passionately committed to their cause and, because most of the battles were fought in the South, knew the land better. After huge casualties on both sides, the North (Yankees) won. Even so, newly emancipated (freed) slaves were not always accepted even in the North, and Lincoln's reforms were not popular everywhere. Abolishing slavery, and the attitudes surrounding it, proved easier to do in theory than in practice. Some people would say that many of the old attitudes and beliefs still linger on, even today.

To church in Uncle Hammer's car

The family's preparations for attending church are an example of Mrs Logan's comment to Cassie about the importance of people making the best of their lives. (Notice that the way Cassie regards her mother is subtly emphasised by the description of her hair before she shapes it.) Against this background of making do, Hammer gives Stacey a new wool coat as an advance Christmas present. Although Stacey feels too grown up now to give Hammer a hug, and shakes hands instead, the way he gives the coat away will show that he still has a lot of maturing to do yet.

What makes Stacey sulk?

Stacey

Hammer's car and Stacey's new coat create a strong impression at church, although T.J.'s reaction to the coat is typically envious. Why does Stacey feel so hurt by T.J's comments? Cassie clearly wants to prevent T.J. getting a ride in Hammer's new car, as punishment for insulting Stacey and, probably, because the rest of the children do not like him. But why, when Mama suggests that T.J. might like a ride, does Cassie speak up 'before Stacey could reply', and what does it say about Stacey's maturity that he 'sulked' all the way home?

'A black man's life ain't worth the life of a cowfly down here.'

On their journey home, Hammer frightens Mama and Big Ma by his talk of burning the Wallace store. What 'other way' do you think Mama has in mind to deal with the Wallaces? Hammer's impetuous character cannot resist the temptation of getting one up on the Wallace family when they meet at the bridge. As an ex-soldier of World War I, Hammer's victory over the Wallaces at Soldiers Bridge is perhaps fitting – and an omen for the future – but Mama knows that one day they will have to pay for it. Hammer's victory will be all the more galling for the Wallaces because the right-of-way rule seems to be regularly broken if black families are on the bridge first; and because they mistook him for Harlan Granger, who seems to occupy the top position in the local pecking order of importance, whilst we already know that 'nigras' are at the bottom.

■ Self-test (Questions) Chapters 4–6

Uncover the plot

Delete two of the three alternatives given, to find the correct plot. Beware possible misconceptions and muddles.

The children learn from Mama/Mr Wallace/T.J. that the night men have burnt/tarred and feathered/beaten Mr Tatum after he accused the preacher/Mr Granger/Mr Barnett of being a liar. T.J. cheats in a test at school but Stacey/Cassie/Mama ends up getting the blame. Mr Morrison breaks up the resulting fight between T.J. and Little Man/Stacey/Cassie. The children are taken to visit Mr Tatum/Mr Berry/Mr Morrison to see his injuries. After visiting the market at Vicksburg/Jackson/Strawberry, Big Ma calls to see Mr Barnett/Mr Jamison/Mr Granger and, later, Cassie is humiliated by being forced to apologise to Lillian Jean by Stacey/Mr Morrison/Big Ma. T.J. admires a shotgun/rifle/handgun in the Barnett store. A surprise visit is paid by Uncle Hammer/Papa/Mr Granger, who has brought his new car, but trouble almost develops when he hears about the incident at the market involving Mr Morrison/Mr Simms/Mr Barnett. Mama tells Cassie how her ancestors originally came from Africa/Alabama/Arkansas and Uncle Hammer gives Stacey an early Christmas present of a book/a dog/a coat. On the way back from church the children give the family at a bridge, mistaking them for Uncle Hammer/Mr Tatum/Mr Granger.

Who? What? Why? When? Where? How?

1 Who 'seldom ever cried'?
2 What was Little Man's greatest fear about being tarred and feathered?
3 Who gets a beating for protecting T.J.?
4 Who is caught going through Mama's books, and what are they suspected of?
5 Whose two daughters died when they were young?
6 What did Mama do instead of beating the children for disobeying her by going to the Wallace store, and why?
7 Where does Cassie experience the cruellest day in her life?
8 Who says; 'You look into her eyes and tell me she ain't hurt!' About whom are they speaking, and to whom?
9 Who has dark, red-brown skin, a square-jawed face, high cheekbones and an aloofness which could never quite be bridged by others?

10 How is the right of way supposed to work at Soldiers Bridge, and what often happens instead?
11 Name the three Wallaces.
12 What do the shiny exteriors of Mama's shoes hide?
13 'But they didn't teach us Christianity to save our souls, but to teach us obedience', says Mama to Cassie. Why does Mama think that most white people decided to believe that black people weren't people like everybody else?
14 Why did Papa Luke's owners not try to break him, even though he ran away three times?

More about people

1 Who says 'I already know what I am!', and to whom?
2 What is the relationship between Uncle Hammer and David Logan?
3 Who says – and to whom – that one day they will all have to pay for what happens on the bridge?
4 Which two characters drive the same make of car, and what make is this?
5 In which part of the world were Big Ma's parents, Papa Luke and Mama Rachel, both born?
6 'What we give them is not respect but fear'. Who says this to whom, and who are they talking about?
7 Who do the children meet who has no nose, no hair on their head, scarred skin and wizened black lips, like charcoal?
8 From whom did Grandpa Logan buy his first two hundred acres of land?
9 Who says; 'The opportunity, dear sister, was too much to resist', and when?
10 Who cut down the trees which make the glade where Big Ma goes to sit in the old forest, and when?
11 Against whom does Harlan Granger still hold a grudge because he sold two hundred acres of land to the Logans?
12 How much of Mr Turner's cotton crop money does Mr Montier take as his share?
13 Why do many sharecroppers still not have any money left after they have paid the landowner their share of the cotton crop money?
14 Where does Mama suggest that families shop instead of at the Wallace store?

Self-test (Answers) Chapters 4–6

Uncover the plot

The children learn from T.J. that the night men have tarred and feathered Mr Tatum after he accused Mr Barnett of being a liar. T.J. cheats in a test at school but Stacey ends up getting the blame. Mr Morrison breaks up the resulting fight between T.J. and Stacey. The children are taken to visit Mr Berry to see his injuries. After visiting the market at Strawberry, Big Ma calls to see Mr Jamison and, later, Cassie is humiliated by being forced to apologise to Lillian Jean by Big Ma. T.J. admires a handgun in the Barnett store. A surprise visit is paid by Uncle Hammer, who has brought his new car, but trouble almost develops when he hears about the incident at the market involving Mr Simms. Mama tells Cassie how her ancestors originally came from Africa and Uncle Hammer gives Stacey an early Christmas present of a coat. On the way back from church the Wallaces give way to the family at a bridge, mistaking them for Mr Granger.

Who? What? Why? When? Where? How?

1 Cassie

2 That if it happened to them they would never get clean again

3 Stacey

4 T.J., who is suspected of looking for the answers to the forthcoming tests

5 Big Ma's

6 She took them to visit Mr Berry so that they could see what the Wallaces had done to him

7 In Strawberry

8 Uncle Hammer, who is talking about Cassie to Big Ma

9 Uncle Hammer

10 Whoever is on the bridge first is supposed to have right of way, but often black families had to back off the bridge and give way to white, even though they were already part way across

11 Dewberry, Thurston, and Kaleb

12 The fact that the soles have large holes in them

13 Because slavery became so profitable for white people, whether they actually owned slaves or not

14 Because he had a knowledge of herbs and cures and he tended the slaves and animals on the plantation with his knowledge of medicine

More about people

1 Cassie, talking to Mr Barnett

2 They are brothers

3 Mama, talking to Uncle Hammer

4 Mr Granger and Uncle Hammer both drive a Packard

5 In Mississippi

6 Mama says this to Cassie about white people like Mr Simms

7 Mr Berry

8 Mr Hollenbeck

9 Uncle Hammer, when the Wallaces mistook him for Mr Granger

10 Mr Andersen and his men, who came from Strawberry whilst Papa was away on the railroad

11 Mr Jamison

12 Half

13 The landowner guarantees the credit of his sharecroppers (tenants) at the local stores. For doing this the landowner usually charges about ten to fifteen per cent of what the sharecroppers have spent. The landowner in addition also repays the interest charged by the store as well as the actual amount spent

14 In Vicksburg

Chapter 7

Stacey reveals that he has given his new coat to T.J. and Uncle Hammer says that T.J. may keep it as a punishment for Stacey's stupidity. The children's father returns and the family celebrate. During the evening's conversation Mr Morrison tells the children about his past. After the children have gone to bed all the adults except Mr Morrison continue talking about the Wallace store and are overheard by Cassie, who has woken up. The following morning the children awake to Christmas presents and later an embarrassing moment occurs when Jeremy Simms calls with gifts. The day after Christmas Mr Jamison calls and Big Ma signs over her control of the land to her sons, Hammer and David Logan. Mr Jamison offers to back the credit for any families who wish to shop in Vicksburg instead of at the Wallace store. Mr Granger visits the Logan home and threatens the family with the loss of their land.

Stacey's coat

Uncle Hammer's reaction to the news about the coat is much more frightening than the children would have expected from their father. The placing of this incident just before the arrival of Papa is not accidental – what effect is achieved by this arrangement? (Think about the contrasting characters of Papa and Hammer.)

Mr Logan & Uncle Hammer

How do you react to the reasons which Stacey gives for parting with the coat? What evidence is there to show that Stacey already knows he has been a fool? How does the later incident with the flute show us that he has learnt his lesson?

Papa returns for Christmas

The celebrations, when Papa returns as usual at Christmas, are vividly described and emphasise the happy, warm and loving home which the Logans share. As they gather together 'in the heart of the house' to share food, companionship and fond memories, their comfort, security and happiness contrast strongly with the unhappiness caused by the discrimination and hostility which some of the white community direct at black families, and which has been a feature of the last few chapters. It is this 'other' atmosphere which surfaces again when Jeremy arrives.

Mr Morrison remembers

A sudden change of mood occurs as the evening wears on when Mr Morrison reminisces – almost to himself – about his memories of the past. The contrast with the Logans' memories is very strong. Why does Mildred Taylor have the characters talk at this time in 'hushed' voices? Think of other kinds of occasion when people might talk like this. Look carefully at Mr Morrison's first few words for a clue.

History

'Hammer, you go to burning and we'll have nothing.'

Cassie wakens in the night from her evil dreams of a hell of flames and night  men to overhear the adults discussing what can be done about the Wallace store. Notice how often Mildred Taylor uses this same 'overhearing' device to allow the reader to learn something they otherwise might not. This clever technique also emphasises the often scary mood; the novel is full of terrible deeds, or veiled threats, or other things – many of which are only hinted at by characters, some of which are never to be spoken of at all, whilst others may be discussed only in secret or in low voices. Which thing that Stacey does is never to be spoken of, and which thing does Papa do which is treated in the same way?

Cassie

Books!

The presents of books stresses the importance of education in the Logan household, and is a reminder of Mama's profession – but notice the difference between this occasion and the time at the school when books were given out. How was the sort of education the school books were intended to give very different to what the children will learn from these? To help you with this, look at Papa's comments about these treasured Christmas gifts. If you have yourself read any of the books which the children receive, you should be able to see that they all have something in common with the values which the children's parents are teaching them as they grow up.

History

Jeremy's gift

Jeremy's visit is uncomfortable for almost everyone. Cassie's tactless outburst  about Jeremy's gifts, and Mama's comment about her mouth, remind us that Cassie often speaks first and thinks later. On what other occasion does Cassie's 'mouth' get her into trouble? Notice that Jeremy's gift is something he has made himself – what does this, and his comment 'it ain't much', tell you about the sincerity of his friendship for Stacey? What present have the Logan children given Jeremy?

Cassie

Friendship between black and white

 Stacey rejects T.J.'s nasty comments about his present from Jeremy because he now has T.J.'s measure and can see that T.J. is envious. Stacey realises that Jeremy would be a better friend than T.J. Papa's view of friendship between blacks and whites is realistic but depressing. But look carefully at

T.J. Avery

the reasons Papa gives for his belief, because later on we see that he may be wrong – think about what Mr Jamison does.

An unwelcome Christmas present!

The children are punished for visiting the Wallace store – 'Papa never forgot anything'. Unpleasant though the beating is, why do the children prefer this kind of punishment to the tongue-lashing of Uncle Hammer?

Mr Jamison makes a surprising offer

Following Big Ma's visit to his office in Strawberry, Mr Jamison has called

with the papers to transfer the ownership of the land from her to her two sons. Unexpectedly, Mr Jamison offers to back the credit of families who wish to boycott the Wallace store, because he knows that if the Logans do so they can only offer their land as security. Notice that nobody challenges his assertion that if they did this they would lose the land – what unspoken understanding do they all have?

Land ownership (If the Logans put their land up as security think about what Harlan Granger would certainly do.) Mr Jamison is a lawyer with a high regard for justice; how does this explain why he and his wife have made this offer? Notice what he says about the Wallaces.

Mr Granger wastes no time

The visit of Mr Jamison is swiftly followed by one from Harlan Granger. A

clue to Uncle Hammer's dedication to their ownership of the land is given when we see that it is he who swiftly responds to Harlan Granger's threat about the loan with 'Ain't gonna lose it'. Hammer will later sell all he owns, even the car which so clearly irritates Harlan Granger (why?), to back the loan. Papa says nothing until the end, letting Hammer keep goading Harlan Granger with the truth. Harlan Granger is obviously not used to being spoken to in this forthright and honest way, as we can see from his 'harsh' voice and the way his face 'paled'. In contrast, Papa's voice is 'very quiet, very distinct, very sure', and he 'impaled' their visitor with his stare. We may feel that Mr Jamison was right and that the Logans cannot win. We may even agree that all Papa can do is 'want these children to know we tried'. But if Harlan Granger had been so sure of victory, would he have bothered to come to the Logans to try to make them change their minds?

Chapter 8

Uncle Hammer leaves and Cassie takes to carrying Lillian Jean's books to school, to the amazement of the other children. T.J. is caught cheating in the examinations. Cassie lures Lillian Jean away from the main road on the way home from school, gives her a beating and makes her apologise for mistreating her. Mr Granger and other members of the school board visit Mama's class at school, following which she is fired. It becomes clear that T.J. is the cause of the school board's visit and he is avoided by the other students at school.

'God wants all his children to do what's right.'

The last two chapters have been about people's thoughts and plans. The

Cassie

action of the book now resumes with Cassie's revenge on 'Miz' Lillian Jean. She gets good advice from Papa, who treats her like an adult when he advises her that it is up to her to decide what things in life she cannot back down on. Papa's comment also explains Stacey's earlier caution about the wrecking of the bus – whatever Cassie does, there must be no come-back from Mr Simms. Look how his comment that people have to have self-respect also

explains Mr Jamison's reasons for offering to back their credit. Papa's words are an echo of Cassie's ironic comment to Lillian Jean; 'that's what I'm gonna do from now on. Just what I gotta.' Later, following her beating at Cassie's hands, it is clear that Lillian Jean never understood what hit her. From being someone who blurts out inappropriate comments, Cassie has now become someone who can hold her tongue – even in the face of outrage from her younger brothers and sneers from T.J. But notice Stacey's comment: 'This here thing's between Cassie and Lillian Jean…' Whose words do you hear echoed from a previous occasion here? (Hint: it followed a fight.) Do you think Stacey guesses what's going on?

'She did it on purpose!' T.J. accused, a nasty scowl twisting his face.

T.J. flees after being caught cheating by Mama. The visit of the school board

History

seems unconnected at the time, but later we learn that T.J. is responsible for this, and for Mama being fired as a result. Again, we witness the classroom scene through the eyes of Cassie, who is watching when she should be elsewhere. Significantly, two of the neighbourhood's biggest bigots – Harlan Granger and Kaleb Wallace – accuse Mama of doing wrong by teaching the truth about slavery as opposed to the distorted version of events written in the 'white'

books approved by the Board of Education.

Mildred Taylor carefully avoids stereotyping all whites in the novel as racist and all blacks as good. Notice how Mr Wellever, the principal, gives her no support – like Miss Crocker he also, perhaps, regards Mama as a 'maverick'.

The day, which had begun with a victory for Cassie, ends with a defeat for Mama, underlining how vulnerable they are to the likes of Mr Granger. But Mama and the family take this with dignity. Mr Morrison offers to find work, and Papa says they will plant more cotton. Papa explains to the children the size of the sacrifice that Mama has had to make for her belief in justice.

The meaning of the land

On several occasions Big Ma, Mama and Papa go down to the pasture, or to the trees, when they want to think. Under what kind of circumstances do they do this, and why are the pasture or the trees appropriate places for them to go? If this seems a difficult point, carefully re-read what Big Ma says in Chapter 4 about what the land means to her.

Land ownership

'Y'all can't just turn on me just 'cause–'

When the truth comes out about T.J.'s part in Mama being sacked, Stacey does not beat him as Little Man expects. Stacey has learned that there are worse punishments. This is an important moment in the story and is skilfully handled by Mildred Taylor. There is dramatic irony in what Stacey says, because his prophetic remark is true in a way he does not himself appreciate. We know that at the end of the book 'what he got coming to him is worse than a beating'.

Stacey

When he gets back to school T.J. is shunned by the other students for what he has done. He is astonished by this. Which other character has reacted similarly to getting their come-uppance, and in what way are these two characters alike?

The character of T.J.

T.J. shouts after the children that he has better friends than them, white friends. But you should recall Papa's observation to Stacey on Christmas Day (when Jeremy called) that 'you see blacks hanging 'round with whites, they're headed for trouble'. Significantly, T.J.'s empty jibes 'faded into the wind'.

T.J. Avery

By now we see that T.J. is untrustworthy and boastful. He will abuse his family and friends and has no respect for anyone. He is completely self-centred and a cheat, and fails to make anything of his own education. He is also very jealous. Why is it that his character has turned out like this, do you suppose, whilst the Logan children have turned out differently? If you can decide why this is, see if your reasoning also explains why Jeremy Simms is the kind of person he is (this is harder, and you may want to check the character outlines at the start of this Guide to help you).

Chapter 9

It is spring and T.J. is keeping company with Lillian Jean's elder brothers Melvin and R.W. who, according to Jeremy, make fun of him behind his back. It seems as though T.J. is heading for certain trouble. Papa says he must leave to return to his work on the railroad. Mr Avery and Mr Lanier call to say that they will have to return to shopping at the Wallace store because Mr Granger is demanding more money and threatening to evict them from their land. Seven families continue to boycott the store, but on their return from shopping for them in Vicksburg, Papa, Stacey and Mr Morrison are attacked by the Wallaces. During the attack Papa is shot and his leg broken, although Mr Morrison badly hurts two of the Wallaces.

T.J. is a figure of fun to the Simms brothers

T.J. Avery

When Jeremy Simms wishes he could see the children more often, the inferior education of blacks is again emphasised by the much shorter school year they have. Stacey cannot understand why Jeremy does not like 'his own kin', but Cassie can. This underlines the difference between the warm and loving Logan family and that of the Simms or Wallaces. Jeremy's brothers Melvin and R.W. are obviously taking advantage of T.J., whom they regard as a figure of fun. Like Cassie, we probably cannot imagine that T.J. is 'dumb' enough not to know this, but Mama explains the real reason for T.J.'s behaviour. We have seen Mama's keen insight into the character of others before – remember her explanation to Cassie of why Mr Simms behaved that way he did in Strawberry. In their treatment of T.J., R.W. and Melvin are behaving very like their father, and for the same reasons. The Simms seem to need to bully others to bolster their own poor self-esteem.

A feast of butterbeans and cornbread

Compare the meal the family have here with the festivities at Christmas. Although that was a special time, the contrast clearly shows how far they are having to tighten their belts – but Papa treats it as a feast. The visit of their loyal friend Mr Jamison hints at further trouble ahead and helps to build the tension in the story, together with Papa's 'gut feeling' that the trouble isn't over yet.

Mr Lanier and Mr Avery call with bad news

Papa's intuition is proved correct when Mr Avery and Mr Lanier arrive to say

Mr Logan & Uncle Hammer

that they have been bullied into shopping at the Wallace store again. Mr Granger says he will raise his share of their crop to sixty per cent. In addition the Wallaces have threatened to call in their store debts and have them put on the chain gang (a form of prison slave-labour where men were chained together in teams to work in harsh conditions on roads, railways, etc.). Papa is angered at Stacey's comments when the men have left. He explains that Stacey was 'born blessed' with ownership of land and that if he had not been he would, like families such as the Laniers and the Averys, 'cry out for it while you try to survive'. Cassie's crying for the land at the end of the novel is, like the incident here, another reminder of the meaning of the book's title and the central importance of land ownership. Notice how, later on, Papa's words to Cassie echo those of hers to Lillian Jean in Chapter 8: 'We keep doing what we gotta…'

Papa, Mr Morrison and Stacey go to Vicksburg for the shopping

Stacey

Papa has included Stacey because he wants him to learn to take care of things, to grow up 'strong… not a fool like T.J.' Mama emphasises the importance of education when she says that Stacey has 'more brains and learning than that'. Again, we hear this conversation via the eavesdropping Cassie. Mama and Papa have very differing views about how good a parent to T.J. Mr Avery is being – which of them do you think is right?

The storm breaks

As Papa, Stacey and Mr Morrison are due to return from Vicksburg, it begins

Racism & Justice

to rain. The rumbling thunder foreshadows the events to come and the conversation in the Logan household becomes increasingly tense as the return of the wagon becomes overdue. The household has become the centre of a storm in several senses, and when Papa returns, shot and with a broken leg, it is clear that Stacey has seen more growing up than Papa had in mind. Their wagon was sabotaged by two boys (the Simms, perhaps?) in Vicksburg and during their return in the storm they were attacked in the dark whilst fixing it. Papa was shot and the wagon rolled over his leg, breaking it. The family's guardian angel, the giant Mr Morrison, faced their three attackers and badly injured two of them. It is clear that the attackers were the Wallaces. Stacey's too-quick denial of his brother's fear that their father will die shows how frightening he found the experience.

53

War has been declared on the Logans

Harlan Granger has had Mama sacked (with the unwitting help of T.J.) and the boycott of the store has largely collapsed following threats from him and the Wallaces. But the Wallaces have paid a high price for trying to get even with the Logans – one of them almost certainly has a broken back, another a broken arm, and they have been humiliated by being defeated in spite of having firearms and outnumbering Mr Morrison three to one. But the Logans have also paid a high price. The loss of Mama's salary has jeopardised their ability to pay the mortgage on the land – opening up the threat from Harlan Granger to take their land from them. And now Papa has almost been killed and will not be able to work on the railroad because of his broken leg, further endangering their future and their ownership of the land.

■ Self-test (Questions) Chapters 7–9

Uncover the plot

Delete two of the three alternatives given, to find the correct plot. Beware possible misconceptions and muddles.

Stacey gets in trouble because of his lying/coat/temper. Papa/Mr Morrison/Mr Avery arrives the day before Christmas and there is much celebrating, during which Mr Morrison tells the story of how his children/wife/parents, who lived in a shantytown outside Shreveport, were beaten/murdered/robbed by night men. After Christmas dinner the children receive a surprise visit from Jeremy Simms/Mr Granger/Uncle Hammer, who has brought gifts. Big Ma signs over the land to her two sons and Mr Granger/Mr Jamison/Mr Hollenbeck offers to back the credit of local families who wish to shop in Vicksburg. Kaleb Wallace/Harlan Granger/Mr Andersen calls and threatens the family with the loss of their land if they continue to cause him trouble. Cassie bribes/makes friends with/carries food for Lillian Jean and then humiliates her with a secret beating in the woods. Stacey/Cassie/T.J. is caught cheating again in the examinations but gains revenge by getting Mama/Miss Crocker/Mr Wellever fired. Mr Lanier and Mr Avery/Mr Wallace/Mr Grimes call to say that they must return to shopping at the Wallace store because of loyalty to/threats from/bribes sent by the whites. Papa/Mr Morrison/Mr Jamison is shot and his leg broken in a fight with the Wallaces one night, returning from shopping in Strawberry/Jackson/Vicksburg.

Who? What? Why? When? Where? How?

1 What, according to Mr Morrison, were 'breeded stock'?
2 How old was Mr Morrison when his parents died?
3 Who would prefer to deal with the Wallaces by burning them out?
4 What presents did the children receive on Christmas day?
5 What event happened in the barn the day after Christmas?
6 Which family shared Christmas dinner at the Logans' home?
7 Who had a face so placid that it was difficult to guess what thought lay behind it?
8 Who gave friendship and from whom did they receive a flute in return?

9 According to Mr Jamison, what is it that Harlan Granger absolutely will not permit?
10 Whose temper nearly flew out of their mouth but they forced it to stay inside, and when?
11 Name three of Mama's visitors to her history lesson.
12 What changes occur in Mama's baking style after she is fired?
13 Which of the local landowners do and do not raise their demands for their share of the cotton crop?
14 What, according to Papa, is the lesson to be learned from the fig tree?

Who is this?

1 Who said that a man should not blame others for his own stupidity?
2 How old are Jeremy's brothers R.W. and Melvin?
3 Who says that one day maybe blacks and whites can be real friends, but not right now?
4 Who is told that nobody's respect is worth more than their own, and by whom?
5 Who accuses the Averys and the Laniers of behaving like scared jackrabbits?
6 Who got so sick he couldn't discipline his son?
7 Who is suspected of tampering with the wheels on the wagon?
8 Who says 'It's my fault his leg's busted!'?
9 Who was flung down on the ground so hard it may have broken his back?
10 Who learns the hard way that some people will always try to talk you out of a good thing if you already have it?
11 Who stole watermelons from Mr Ellis, and when?
12 Which things did the children need to know, because it was their history?
13 Who had a grudging respect for Mr Jamison and why?
14 Who accused whom of thinking himself too good to work in the fields like other folks?

Self-test (Answers) Chapters 7–9

Uncover the plot

Stacey gets in trouble because of his coat. Papa arrives the day before Christmas and there is much celebrating, during which Mr Morrison tells the story of how his parents, who lived in a shantytown outside Shreveport, were murdered by night men. After Christmas dinner the children receive a surprise visit from Jeremy Simms, who has brought gifts. Big Ma signs over the land to her two sons and Mr Jamison offers to back the credit of local families who wish to shop in Vicksburg. Harlan Granger calls and threatens the family with the loss of their land if they continue to cause him trouble. Cassie makes friends with Lillian Jean and then humiliates her with a secret beating in the woods. T.J. is caught cheating again in the examinations but gains revenge by getting Mama fired. Mr Lanier and Mr Avery call to say that they must return to shopping at the Wallace store because of threats from the whites. Papa is shot and his leg broken in a fight with the Wallaces one night returning from shopping in Vicksburg.

Who? What? Why? When? Where? How?

1 Slaves bred together to produce more slaves for selling, especially after the government outlawed bringing any more slaves from Africa
2 Barely six years old
3 Uncle Hammer
4 Books, licorice, oranges, bananas and clothes
5 The children are given a beating by their father for going to the Wallace store
6 The Avery family
7 Mr Jamison
8 Stacey receives a flute from Jeremy Simms in return for his friendship
9 The idea that the Wallaces should be punished just as if they had killed a white man, because that would denote equality between blacks and whites

Who is this?

1 Uncle Hammer
2 Eighteen or nineteen
3 Papa
4 Cassie is told this by Papa
5 Stacey
6 Mr Avery
7 Two boys in Vicksburg, possibly the Simms brothers
8 Stacey
9 One of the Wallaces who attacked the wagon
10 Stacey
11 Papa and Uncle Hammer, when they were young
12 Papa said they needed to know about the way blacks have been badly treated by whites
13 Uncle Hammer, because he was honest about why even the whites who were sympathetic to the blacks wouldn't help them
14 Mr Granger accuses Uncle Hammer of this

10 Cassie, when T.J. accused her of 'Uncle Tomming' Lillian Jean
11 Kaleb Wallace, Harlan Granger, and Mr Wellever
12 She uses less ingredients
13 Mr Granger and Mr Montier do, but Mr Harrison does not
14 That everyone should keep doing what they have to do and not give up in the face of difficulty

Chapter 10

A week has passed since the shooting of Papa. On their return from visiting a local family Mr Morrison and the children are stopped by Kaleb Wallace's truck blocking the road. Kaleb Wallace threatens Mr Morrison for the beating he gave the ambushers, but Mr Morrison lifts the truck out of the way and drives on. August comes and Mr Morrison returns from Strawberry, where he has made the August mortgage payment, with a letter from the bank demanding the full debt be paid. Papa suspects Harlan Granger's hand in this. During the August celebrations Uncle Hammer arrives with the money needed to pay off the mortgage, which he has raised by selling his possessions – including his car – and borrowing money. T.J. arrives at church one day with R.W. and Melvin, hoping to impress the children – but without success.

Times become harder

Although times are obviously hard, Papa is reluctant to ask Hammer for

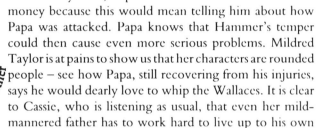

money because this would mean telling him about how Papa was attacked. Papa knows that Hammer's temper could then cause even more serious problems. Mildred Taylor is at pains to show us that her characters are rounded people – see how Papa, still recovering from his injuries, says he would dearly love to whip the Wallaces. It is clear to Cassie, who is listening as usual, that even her mild-mannered father has to work hard to live up to his own high standards. This is an important point which the novel makes several times – having civilised standards means working at it, whilst taking the easy way out produces characters like the Wallaces, R.W., Melvin, or T.J.

Dewberry and Thurston Wallace are still laid up from the beating Mr Morrison gave them, and Dewberry's back is reportedly broken. Although the Wallaces got what they deserved, Mama worries for Mr Morrison's safety.

Mr Morrison lifts Kaleb Wallace's truck

It tells us a lot about the character of whites like Kaleb Wallace that even

History

though it was his family which carried out the cowardly attack on Papa, he is the one who feels that he has been wronged. But he is a cowardly man unless backed by a crowd and a loaded gun. He is speechless and pales with fear when he thinks he might be attacked, but instead Mr Morrison uses his phenomenal strength to gently lift the truck out of the way. Notice how Mr Morrison checks to make sure there is no gun in the truck. On what other occasion has a white character 'paled' when confronted by others in the black community who have a measured determination not to be bullied? In Chapter 7 we learnt about how Mr Morrison's family were taken from him when he was six. Now he feels part of the Logan family, and this is why he does not want to leave them in their time of greatest need.

Why are the Wallaces not in jail for what they did?

Cassie finds the complicated way of things confusing, but Mama explains why it is safer for them not to make a fuss about the attack of the Wallaces. The Wallaces and other like-minded whites will now be at their most dangerous, because until now they have been used to getting their own way all the time. Mama points out that these are now dangerous times.

Racism & Justice

Jeremy sleeps in a tree

Jeremy is always offering friendship, without any strings attached. Notice here how he takes rejection in his stride and is never put off for long. He tells the astonished children about how he has built his bedroom up a tree. Why do you think he likes to pretend that he can see the Logan place from his tree? Think about what Jeremy's sleeping in his tree-home tells you about how comfortable he feels with his own family.

The bank demands the loan money back immediately

Papa correctly sees the malicious hand of Harlan Granger in the bank's sudden demand that the loan be repaid in full – even though, legally, the mortgage gives them four more years to pay it off. This is evidence of Harlan's need to show them 'where they stand in the scheme of things'. Notice what Papa says about taking the matter to court. Why do you suppose he 'laughed dryly' at this idea?

Land ownership

The revival celebrations begin

The celebrations which accompany the annual church revival form a powerful contrast to the troubles and aggression surrounding the black community. These occasions are a celebration of the spiritual unity of the larger black family to which they all belong, a time of sharing and of hope in spite of their struggles. Significantly, T.J. attends the revival as an outcast, whilst Hammer appears as a saving angel with the money the family needs. Think about what Hammer has been prepared to sacrifice for what he says is important in life. Hammer has given up all those things which were not important and returns to Chicago penniless. T.J., however, sees his happiness in terms of things like a pearl-handled gun.

'It's gonna storm all right... but it may not come till late on over in the night.'

Papa's words here are prophetic, for the climax of the book's action is drawing rapidly closer. As the storm gathers, T.J. arrives, accompanied by R.W. and Melvin Simms – two symbols of all that threatens the black community. His shallow values are emphasised by the way he thinks that the

important things in life are having fancy new clothes (remember Stacey's coat?), and being given the pearl-handled pistol. It becomes clear that the Simms brothers have only come with T.J. as part of an agreement that he will then do something they want.

Symbolically, the Logan children turn their backs on these 'white devils' and go into church. T.J. is left, lonely and pathetic, stranded in the darkness between his own people in the church and the insistent hooting of the horn of the white boys' truck. Fatefully, T.J. yet again makes the wrong decision.

Growing up

Chapter 11

Late one night T.J. comes to the house and asks the children for help. He, R.W. and Melvin have stolen the pearl-handled pistol from the Barnetts' store. During the robbery R.W. left both Mr and Mrs Barnett unconscious when they discovered the boys in the store. When T.J. said he was going to tell everybody what the other two had done, they beat him badly, so he escaped. The children help T.J. to get home, but on their way back they see several vehicles arrive at the Avery home and noisy, angry men leap out. The men drag Mr and Mrs Avery outside and beat their children, and the stolen pistol is discovered. R.W. and Melvin have told everyone that T.J. and two other black boys committed the robbery. Only the arrival of Mr Jamison, followed by the sheriff, saves T.J. from being hung at once, but the men threaten to take him elsewhere and hang him, together with Papa and Mr Morrison. The children run to tell Papa what is happening.

Roll of thunder, hear my cry

The night is full of distant thunder as Mr Morrison sits as usual, watching and waiting, and chants his song of defiance. His behaviour is another of those things which Cassie knows are never spoken of, although she is certain she knows why he watches and waits. Mr Morrison knows that, like the approaching storm, events are building rapidly to a climax. He waits in the certain knowledge that trouble is coming. Notice the significant use of the word 'chant' to describe his singing of the song from which the book gets its title.

History

Why has Mildred Taylor used this word, do you think? Look carefully at the words of the song. Consider what else is usually chanted, and what this tells you about Mr Morrison's role in the story.

An unexpected guest arrives

During the night a distressed T.J. arrives. He has been beaten and threatened by his white 'friends' R.W. and Melvin Simms. He tells the children he is afraid to go home because his father will throw him out, and that the Simms have threatened him if he tells about the night's events. We learn about the

T.J. Avery

robbery and how the Simms have cleverly taken in T.J. Notice that although T.J. is not the one who has committed the violence against the Barnetts, the Simms covered their faces so that they will be taken for blacks. So whilst they remain unknown, T.J.'s face was plainly visible and because of the pistol he is the one with evidence which incriminates him. After the robbery the Simms have gone to the pool hall, probably to fix up an alibi, and left the beaten T.J. in the wagon. He has made his painful way home, avoiding the Simms' place out of fear of further beatings. T.J. has realised far too late that his only true friend has been Stacey.

The storm breaks

The thunder, like a wild animal stalking its prey, is 'creeping closer now,

Racism & Justice

rolling angrily over the forest depths and bringing the lightning with it', as the children take the injured T.J. home and watch him climb into the house through a side window. The 'lightning' is indeed approaching, as half a dozen vehicles suddenly appear and flood the unsuspecting Avery house with their headlights. An angry mob of men – including R.W. and Melvin Simms – storm the house and drag the family out and severely attack them. They have come for T.J. and their savagery upsets the Logan children. But Stacey knows that for their own safety they must not be discovered. The Simms brothers have pinned everything on T.J. who, stupidly, still has the pistol on him.

Mr Jamison appears with the sheriff

Why is there 'an embarrassed silence' when Mr Jamison arrives? Look at how he reacts to the men's threats. Who else reacts to threats in a calm, unruffled manner, and do the two men have anything else in common?

'A crescendo of ugly hate rose from the men …'

The behaviour of the sheriff, who acts 'as if he would rather not be here at

Racism & Justice

all' tells us where his loyalties lie and contrasts with that of the brave Mr Jamison. The sheriff has no words of his own to speak, he is only a messenger for Harlan Granger, who obviously does not care what happens so long as it is not on his land. Notice that although the sheriff represents the law, Mr Jamison represents justice. We have already seen, on many occasions, that the two are not the same.

Mr Jamison rushes to defend T.J. from immediate hanging. As the mob talk of getting Papa and Mr Morrison to hang also, Cassie leaves Stacey at the Avery house, takes her younger brothers and agrees to go home and get Papa. As they make their way home the thunder 'crashed against the corners of the world'. We never see T.J. again.

The storm has been building throughout the novel and its unleashing now increases the dramatic tension of the action. The white lightning 'split the sky' in the same way the violence of the whites threatens to destroy the children's world.

Chapter 12

Papa and Mr Morrison go out to protect the family, retrieve Stacey and try to save T.J. from the mob. A fire breaks out in the Logans' fields next to Mr Granger's forest and all the men, helped by local farmers, Mama and Big Ma, work together all night to put it out. The Logans lose a quarter of their cotton crop. News arrives that Mr Barnett has died from his injuries and that T.J. has been arrested and may be hanged.

Papa will do what he has to do

When Papa hears about what is taking place at the Averys', he swiftly moves to help, but Mama pleads with him not to use the gun. As Papa looks out into the night the lightning again splits the sky – a symbol of the violence erupting all around them. Papa's mysterious reply 'Perhaps...' gives us no clue as to how he will resolve the difficult situation. His determination is shown when he again says that he will do what he has to do, a phrase which, as we have seen, sums up the courage of the Logans. Papa knows that, like Stacey earlier on, he must help T.J., whether the boy is a fool or not.

Mr Logan & Uncle Hammer

The community comes together to save the land

After Papa departs the family see their cotton on fire and everything else is forgotten in their rush to save it. Notice what Big Ma says about what started the fire. The children are frightened because Papa and Stacey are in the trees towards which the fire is spreading. They are told not to go out, and Mama and Big Ma go to help put out the fire. Later, Stacey arrives. He has been concerned about them and has been with his father fighting the fire like everyone else. Jeremy does not realise why all the men were already there, but he tells them that they have all been fighting the fire. The knowledge that they all depend on the land has put other things aside whilst everyone co-operates to help to save the crops and forests.

Land ownership

The destruction of the land

Following the sudden heavy downpour, the fire is put out and the children witness the charred and desolate landscape. The destruction of the land echoes what the mob were set to do to their community. The children find a 'flood' of people working to put out the last of the fire. They are moving slowly, as if sleepwalking, like strange robots. Notice how everyone – from the bigoted Harlan Granger to the vicious Kaleb Wallace – is helping, 'each oblivious of the other'. In what other way have many of the local community been living like this for a long time, in a kind of dream, behaving like robots, not really seeing the people around them?

What happened?

Stacey and Mama know what Papa did – he set the fire deliberately, sacrificing some of their cotton crop, to save the situation. When Cassie asks Stacey why Mr Morrison arrived at the Averys' place without Papa, he deliberately offers a reason which they all see cannot be true. Cassie shows how much she has matured by voicing her concern about whether they will have enough money to pay the taxes – she sees that the land not only supports and feeds them, but that it is a symbol of black freedom from oppression, and of hope for the future.

Growing up

News about the robbery

Stacey tells the others about Mr Jamison's bravery in stopping the mob, at risk to his own life, and how Harlan Granger intervened and ordered T.J. to be turned over to Mr Jamison only when his own land was at risk. When Mr Jamison is overheard talking to Papa and Mr Morrison, we hear that Mr Barnett has died – so the charge against T.J. is likely to be one of murder.

The truth about the fire

Mr Jamison has obviously realised what has really happened to start the fire, but he leaves this unspoken, advising Papa to stay clear of things for a while. Cassie realises that Papa started the fire, but that this is another of those 'known and unknown things, never to be spoken' and she tells us that her glance at Stacey revealed that she 'knew, and understood the meaning of what I knew'.

I cried for T.J. For T.J. and the land.

T.J.'s ominous comment that he would sell his life for the pearl-handled pistol seems to be coming true, as Papa's answers to the children's questions make clear. Papa says that whilst it may have to be that way, 'it shouldn't be'. This is a central theme which runs through the novel. Cassie sees that T.J. is unlikely to get justice at his trial, and that even though it is almost 150 years after the American Constitution declared that all men were created equal, for many blacks this is still a hope for the future, not a present reality. She knows that the struggle must go on, but has learned how and when she should fight and when she should remain silent. She understands the importance of the land and her place in her inheritance. And she has learned to feel sorrow for the sacrifices that dignity, self-respect and freedom will continue to demand of them all.

Racism & Justice

Self-test (Questions) Chapters 10–12

Uncover the plot

Delete two of the three alternatives given, to find the correct plot. Beware possible misconceptions and muddles.

Papa is leaving/getting better/getting worse but money is still tight, so Mr Morrison/Mama/Stacey is out looking for work. Returning from helping Mr Avery/Mr Wiggins/Mr Granger, Mr Morrison meets Kaleb Wallace/Mr Jamison/Mr Barnett, who blocks the road with his truck, but Papa/Uncle Hammer/Mr Morrison lifts it out of the way and drives on. The children hear that T.J. is spending a lot of time with the Granger/Barnett/Simms brothers and is falling into bad ways. Harlan Granger/Kaleb Wallace/Mr Jamison is suspected of being behind the bank's demand for the loan to be repaid/increased/frozen. At the revival meeting in winter/spring/August Uncle Hammer pays a surprise visit, bringing with him the food/money/car the family need. After being involved in a robbery at the Barnett store, Jeremy/Stacey/T.J. is caught when his accomplices, the Simms/Avery/Granger brothers, turn him in to escape detection themselves. In order to protect the family and the Averys from prosecution/the sheriff/hanging, Papa starts a fight/fire/party. The tension and anger is defused as everyone celebrates/ignores/deals with this, but Mama/Papa/Cassie weeps for the unfairness of events.

Who? What? Why? When? Where? How?

1 Why does Papa not want Uncle Hammer to find out that he is injured?
2 Why is Mama afraid for Mr Morrison?
3 Why does Kaleb Wallace not attack Mr Morrison when he meets him on the road?
4 Why does Papa not report the Wallaces for what they did and have them thrown in jail by the sheriff?
5 What is in the envelope which Mr Morrison brings back from Strawberry?
6 Harlan Granger wants the Logans' land. What other need drives him to get the bank to recall their loan?
7 Why are the Simms brothers mistaken for blacks when they rob the Barnetts store?
8 Which individual's actions directly result in the injuries to Mr and Mrs Barnett?
9 How does T.J. get into his house after being taken home by the children?
10 How do fire and water between them avert two disasters?
11 Who suggests that the mob hang Papa and Mr Morrison?
12 Who has their bedroom up in a tree?
13 How do the men hope to prevent the fire from spreading?
14 What piece of evidence is produced to implicate T.J. in the robbery?

People are judged by what they do

1 What happens to T.J. after the fire?
2 'It can't grow cotton. You can't build a home on it. And you can't raise four fine babies in it.' Who is this talking, and what about?
3 What 'difference' does T.J. hope it will make to things when he brings R.W. and Melvin Simms with him to the revival, and why is he so disappointed with the reaction he gets?
4 Who says: 'Y'all decide to hold court out here tonight?', and to whom?
5 What is the real meaning of the message which the sheriff brings from Mr Granger?
6 'Since when did you start worrying about taxes?' Who says this and to whom?
7 What eventually happens to Mr Barnett and when?
8 Why do people think the fire started in the cotton field, and how did it really start?
9 Who orders the mob to fight the fire and why?
10 Who 'backed away, silent, not wanting to believe, but believing still', and from what did they back away?
11 Why does Cassie have feelings for T.J. even though she has never liked him?
12 For which two things does Cassie cry at the end of the book?
13 Cassie says that Stacey 'saw in my eyes that I knew, and understood the meaning of what I knew...' What is this special thing which Cassie has come to know?
14 Who, according to some of the local folk, got what was coming to him, as far as Mr Jamison can tell?

Self-test (Answers) Chapters 10–12

Uncover the plot

Papa is getting better but money is still tight, so Mr Morrison is out looking for work. Returning from helping Mr Wiggins, Mr Morrison meets Kaleb Wallace, who blocks the road with his truck, but Mr Morrison lifts it out of the way and drives on. The children hear that T.J. is spending a lot of time with the Simms brothers and is falling into bad ways. Harlan Granger is suspected of being behind the bank's demand for the loan to be repaid. At the revival meeting in August Uncle Hammer pays a surprise visit, bringing with him the money the family need. After being involved in a robbery at the Barnett store, T.J. is caught when his accomplices, the Simms brothers, turn him in to escape detection themselves. In order to protect the family and the Averys from hanging, Papa starts a fire. The tension and anger is defused as everyone deals with this, but Cassie weeps for the unfairness of events.

Who? What? Why? When? Where? How?

1 Because he does not want to risk Uncle Hammer's temper if he finds out what the Wallaces have done

2 Because people may seek revenge for what he did to Thurston and Dewberry Wallace

3 Because he is the cowardly kind of person who can only act when he has a lot of other people backing him up, plus a loaded gun

4 Because as long as the Wallaces remain embarrassed by their injuries they will not make an official complaint about Mr Morrison attacking white men, which could result in Mr Morrison being sentenced to the chain gang or worse

5 A letter from the bank demanding immediate settlement of the loan on the land

6 He feels that he needs to show the Logans where they stand in the scheme of things as he sees it. He wants to try to show everyone that blacks are not equal to whites and cannot be like them – by owning their own land, for instance

7 Because they are with T.J., who is black, and their faces are masked with stockings and their hands are gloved. Everyone would assume that all three were therefore black, as few people would expect whites to associate with blacks even in the robbing of a store

8 It is R.W. Simms who is the one who hits Mr Barnett with the axe and then slaps at his wife, who then falls backwards and hits her head

9 He climbs into his room through an open window

10 The fire in the cotton field prevents the mob from hanging the Averys and the Logans and the rainstorm prevents the fire from destroying the forest and the other surrounding lands

11 Kaleb and Thurston Wallace

12 Jeremy Simms

13 By digging a deep trench and then burning the grass left between it and the fire

14 The pearl-handled pistol

People are judged by what they do

1 The sheriff and Mr Jamison take him to jail

2 Uncle Hammer is talking about his Packard car, which he has sold to raise money so that the family can repay the loan on their land

3 He hoped that the others would be impressed by the fact that he had white friends, would then think well of him, and would be his friends again. He is disappointed when it does not work because he feels alone and badly wants to be friends again – this is why Cassie almost feels sorry for him

4 Mr Jamison makes this remark to the men who drag the Averys out of their home after the robbery at the Barnett store

5 That Mr Granger does not really care what the men do to the Averys, or any other blacks, but that he will not be implicated by having it happen on his land

6 Mama says this to Cassie

7 He dies at four o'clock on the morning after the robbery

8 People think that lightning struck a fence and set it alight, but in fact Papa started the fire on purpose

9 Mr Granger orders the mob to fight the fire because he is afraid that it will burn his forest

10 Stacey backed away from the knowledge that T.J. will probably hang for murder following the robbery at the Barnett store

11 Because he was always there, always a part of her life, and like all children she had thought that her life would never change

12 She cries for T.J. and for the land

13 That there are some things – like how the fire really started – which are both known and unknown, things which people know but never speak about, not even to close family

14 Papa, when he was lost a quarter of his cotton

Part II

STANDARD MEDICAL TREATMENT

Chapter 6

STATIN WONDERLAND

To paraphrase Oxford professor Sir Rory Collins, statins are just one of life's good things that all of us should be routinely taking, whether or not we are a candidate for heart attack. And the world seems to agree.

In the 30 years since they were launched, annual global sales of statin drugs have grown to around £20 billion ($30.4 billion). One statin, Lipitor (atorvastatin), holds the record as the bestselling drug in history, with annual worldwide sales reaching £6.7 billion ($10.2 billion) in 2008. And in the UK, you don't even have to see a doctor to start your statin regime: there's a version sold in pharmacies you can get without a prescription.

But a major study has revealed that statins are medicine's equivalent of the Emperor's new clothes. Everyone tells us the drug protects against heart disease, but the appalling truth appears to be the exact opposite. Far from being miracle life-savers, statins seem to be a killer for many and helpful to only a small group of people.

So how have doctors got it so wrong? Two factors appear to be at play: the deliberate concealing of the true data; and the disputed theory that LDL cholesterol causes heart disease.

The truth is out there

Two researchers at University College Hospital in Galway, Ireland, uncovered the truth when they analyzed 55 studies of statin therapy. People taking these drugs weren't living longer – and were just as likely to develop heart disease – as people not taking a statin. Worse, women, diabetics and young people were more likely to develop heart disease when taking statins.[1]

And that's the good news, the kind we're allowed to read. Virtually all the research into statins is paid for by their manufacturers – one drug company is spending around £35 million ($53 million) on one study alone – and some have refused to release their data for others to see.

When researchers from the Cochrane Collaboration, an independent research group, analyzed the way statin studies had been presented, they uncovered selective reporting of outcomes and a failure to report adverse reactions, and also that patients who had heart disease had been filtered out of the results.[2]

A drug in search of a disease

The statin story began in 1971 at the laboratories of Japanese pharmaceutical company Sankyo. Biochemist Akira Endo was looking for a compound that could lower cholesterol and be better tolerated than the currently available drugs. As cholesterol is regulated and manufactured in the liver by the enzyme HMG-CoA reductase, Endo reasoned there would be some kind of microorganism that could restrict its development.

He found what he was seeking in the mould *Penicillium citrinum*, from which he developed the chemical agent mevastatin. Although